# A Funny Thing Happened in Prison the Other Day

## Stories from inside an Ohio Prison

**Tom Hattersley**

cover photo: josefkubes/Shutterstock.com

Printed in the United States of America
Published by Braughler Books LLC., Springboro, Ohio

First printing, 2019

ISBN: 978-1-970063-24-0
Library of Congress Control Number: 2019910520

Ordering information: Special discounts are available on quantity purchases by bookstores, corporations, associations, and others. For details, contact the publisher at:

sales@braughlerbooks.com

or at 937-58-BOOKS

For questions or comments about this book, please write to:

info@braughlerbooks.com

**Braughler™**
**Books**
braughlerbooks.com

## Dedication

The work is dedicated to my colleagues
at Pathway Guidance LLC.
Their support helped make this book a reality.

# Contents

# Acknowledgements

I would like to acknowledge my fellow volunteers at Lebanon Correctional Institute. They stepped up to make our world a better place. Thank you to Steve Hendy, Mike Neverman, Pat Neverman, Jon Riley, Bev Smith, Bob Stadler, Pat Steele, and Dave Vandivier.

Thank you to our Program Directors, Marty Arlinghaus and Christine Marallen.

Four friends honored me by reading my early drafts in what I considered to be a feasibility study. Their encouragement was sine qua non to my deciding to publish. Thank you to Benno Duenkelsbuehler, Bill Ernst, Phil Locke and Paul Westrich. Bill Wilken, my fellow Denison Alumni, is to be thanked for badgering me with the idea in the first place.

Thank you to Caitlin Hensel my editor. Thanks to Jan Sabato for her pre-press proofreading.

Most of all, thank you to my spouse, Sharon. I am grateful for her enduring a weekly Wednesday worrying session while I was in prison, for lending her ear to my story ideas, and for her dead-eyed proofreading.

# Prologue

This book grew out of my work at Lebanon Correctional Institute in Ohio meeting with inmates two hours weekly in nine-week sessions over a period of three years. The sessions are named the Prison Response-Ability Project because of my intent to help prison inmates develop the awareness to respond responsibly to life with all of its bumps and bruises rather than react from their wounded cores. Of course, we all need to do so, not just the incarcerated.

I continually get asked why I chose work in prison. Usually with puzzled politeness, but occasionally less politely, such as once, "Why would you want to help those people?!" On the other hand, it has been very fulfilling to have friends and acquaintances stop me in public to tell me how much they appreciate the effort.

I am not precisely sure what motivated me to choose prison work. I can say that, having been educated by Ursuline nuns in grade school and Franciscan brothers and fathers in high school, I was taught early and often the inherent dignity and worth of every human life. And, Mahatma Ghandi's admonition, "A nation's greatness is measured by how it treats its weakest members," resonates with me at a gut level.

However logical our articulated explanations for our behavior and choices, our values and philosophies likely guide us more than we can say. I like to think of life as a great party to which I've been invited through no merit on my part, making me feel like I should show my gratitude by contributing in some way. If, in the end, all I can say is that I gave more than I got, I'll be happy.

I learned about a prison program in California and spent a week—including entering prison for the first time—with the people behind that initiative. I came home determined, developed a curriculum with help from a colleague and went looking for an institution that would accept me. I began volunteering at Lebanon Correctional Institute in Ohio in June of 2016. I entered under the auspices of the Director of Prison Ministries for the Catholic Archdiocese of Cincinnati.

After nearly every Prison Response-Ability Project session, I wrote a post about what I thought might be interesting to people I knew. The primary intent behind the postings has been to humanize the inmates I met and to get us to think about penal policy in the U.S. The idea for organizing the posts into a book came from a friend. He called such a work an ethnographic study.

The title of the book and the titles of the chapters all come from the headings I gave to various posts. I find the book title, A Funny Thing Happened in Prison the Other Day, quite apt when one thinks about the various meanings we give to the word funny.

Of course, there is just plain funny, i.e., causing laughter. That has certainly been true. There is the meaning, amusing. That is also true. I look forward to Wednesday nights sort of like one might look forward to bowling night.

Then there is the meaning of funny, difficult to account for. True again. Funny can mean counterfeit or fraudulent. That speaks for itself. Funny can mean painful ("I've got a funny feeling in my..."), offensive (Don't get funny with...), and, finally, funny can mean contrary to one's expectations. All true.

Over the course of the three years, something funny has happened to me. I have become more and more concerned with two sets of numbers. Firstly, how many millions get imprisoned and how many eventually get released into our neighborhoods. About one out of one hundred American adult males is imprisoned and 95% of those imprisoned get out.

Secondly, how much we spend on imprisoning criminals at the expense of spending money on deterring crime. And, how little we focus on mending the lives of inmates to reduce the 43% incarceration recidivism rate in the U.S.

The U.S. Department of Justice's own website reports a study establishing that policing is a more effective deterrent to crime than long incarceration. Long sentences are expensive, leaving many felons even more felonious. Both the savings from shorter sentences and from eliminating highly expensive death penalty cases could free up funds for more policing and more rehabilitation.

Clearly, we should be talking about this waste of money and lives.

The content of this book is the byproduct of over 130 Facebook and Linkedin postings over a three-year period. I have freely edited those posts to make them more readable in book format.

Just about every Wednesday night when I would return home from prison my wife, Sharon, would ask, "How did it go tonight?" I converted my posts into vignettes thinking of you the reader asking me the same question. Finally, the events and people are real; the names of the people are fictitious.

# CHAPTER 1

# My Experience: Getting into Prison is Hard

*The purpose of life is not to be happy. It is to be useful,*
*to be honorable, to be compassionate, to have it make*
*some difference that you have lived and lived well.*

RALPH WALDO EMERSON

In May 2015, I first entered a prison, three prisons in fact. To say I was anxious is an understatement. I was observing The Enneagram Prison Project sessions for a week in California. We sat in a circle in the prison education room, volunteers mixed among inmates. The inmate next to me was twirling a pencil sharpened on both ends in his fingers in his hand nearest to me. I thought, he could stab me in the neck and kill me. (I think I saw that once on TV.) Then we started talking and, though I still don't know what his offense was, he definitely did not have the disposition of the pencil-in-the-neck murderer that I imagined.

This chapter includes some of my other non-life-threatening prison experiences during my three years of volunteering in weekly two-hour sessions on Wednesday nights at Lebanon Correctional.

## Getting into Prison is Hard
### (POSTED 23 JULY 2016)

Friends have asked about the experience of going into a prison. Here are the steps.

We start with a check-in at the lobby desk; the guard takes your driver's license and looks to see if you are on the approved list (which required paperwork, reference checking and an instructional meeting on, among other topics, how to behave if taken hostage). He issues a visitor's badge and stamps your hand with invisible ink.

On to the second guard in the lobby who screens you just like at the airport, nothing in your pockets, carrying only training materials and driver's license. No cell phone, no money, no food, etc. We walk through the scanner hoping for its silent approval. Finally, pull up your pants legs, pull your pockets inside out, and you are ready to go.

A third guard comes to escort us through the prison security gates to the education room where we work. *Click*, an iron gate rolls open and we walk into a small vestibule with iron bars on both sides. *Thud*, we are locked in. *Click*, a gate rolls open on the other side to another vestibule with iron bars on both sides. *Thud*, we are locked in the second small area.

There, we each show our driver's license and place our invisible-inked hand in a viewer. A fourth guard behind glass checks them. *Click*, the gate rolls open on the other side and we follow our escort out. *Thud*, the gate locks behind us. We proceed down a hall with offices on either side; Warden, Assistant Warden, Major and so on.

We arrive at another double-gated iron bar room. Same sequence, same sounds. The gate rolls open. The gate closes behind. A fifth guard behind glass checks us. The gate opens on the other side. We enter the hallway. The gate behind us rolls to a close with that now familiar *Thud*.

No turning back. We are actually in prison.

We move among the guards and prisoners who are hustling back and forth. We walk about a hundred yards down the hallway. The dining areas are on the right, offices and the chapel on the left. We end up at the education rooms, entering through a locked door past a sixth guard who stays with us as our escort leaves. We wait for our program inmates to arrive.

## A Prisoner Asked, "Why Are You Doing This?"
### (POSTED 13 JULY 2016)

Finishing a session ahead of schedule one week, I asked the inmates if there were any questions. One named Ronald asked skeptically, "Why are you doing this?"

My answer, "For Sister Loretta, for Sister Mary David, for Father Sylvester, for Coach Bacevich, for Professor Morris." Ronald along with every other inmate looked at me with understandable confusion, having no idea about to whom I was referring.

I said, "I have a great life, but I did not get here alone. Those people and many more helped me along the way. Helping you is the best way I can thank them."

Ronald suddenly stood up and moved toward me. Now, I was the one who was confused. I had never been hugged by a convicted felon before.

## Just Saying *No* in Prison
### (POSTED 27 SEPTEMBER 2016)

One can only guess the experience of being a prison guard. Inmates readily complain about how they are treated by them. Catching a little Stockholm Syndrome from the inmates, I started to get annoyed with the guards' treatment of me.

I mean, I'm here to help. I'm a volunteer, and I act like a boy scout compared to what they are used to. For example, friends have donated bags and bags of used books. I lug a bag up every Wednesday evening. The guards always question whether I've cleared the donation with the librarian, sometimes they want paperwork, and sometimes they just say, "No."

Putting myself in the guards' boots, though, I realize a guard will never get in trouble for saying *No*, especially to an inmate. So, *No* is their default setting. *Yes* can get a guard in trouble; *No* won't. Letting an inmate go somewhere in the facility can result in a problem. Keeping an inmate on the cellblock won't.

Nonetheless, the psychology of a pervasive *No* culture has to be damaging to both guards and inmates. One has to come out of prison expecting to hear *No* at every turn.

## Prison Dogs
### (POSTED 17 FEBRUARY 2017)

All of the volunteers and inmates start our two hours in prison together with announcements, birthdays, etc. and then we break up into small groups each run by a volunteer. I try to talk to as many of the total inmate group as I can.

One named Robert is a dog trainer. And, fair to say, a dog lover and lover of having the opportunity to use his prison time meaningfully.

Robert trains young dogs to become service dogs. They live in his cell with him. He has even brought his dogs with him to the sessions.

I have a great niece who has a service dog named Fiona. I thought that she came to my great niece with the name Fiona. So, I asked him if he ever had a Fiona. He said yes.

The following week Robert brought me pictures of his dogs. Fiona is a Golden Retriever, light cream in color, with a distinctively rounded forehead…very endearing, a permanent puppy look. His Fiona was unmistakably the Fiona my great niece got last summer.

Last week I brought a picture of my great niece and Fiona together. I showed the photo to him during our initial gathering. He was thrilled.

I would have loved to give him the picture, but that was not allowed.

At the end of our two hours that night when the inmates went back to their cells, Robert rushed into my classroom to get another look at the photo and asked if I would bring the photo again next week.

## What a Grade School Teacher Taught Me About Prisoners
### (POSTED 10 JULY 2017)

I keep noticing ways that inmates respond just like any other people I might work with out of prison. Starting a new group last week, I used a technique I learned from one of my daughters, a grade school teacher. She advised that beginning with a group by telling the members how talented they are builds positive expectations of themselves and gets more buy-in.

So, I let my new group know that they are—in my opinion—a well above-average group in their level of participation and, more importantly, in their ability to stay on task. (Prison has many distractions to which they can succumb.)

This session was the most productive I've had in my more than a year working in prison. The increased motivation to stay on task, complete the work, and truly listen to one another was palpable.

Lesson to me: my having higher expectations of them caused them to have higher expectations of themselves.

## R-E-S-P-E-C-T in Prison
### (POSTED 5 OCTOBER 2017)

I have been asked how I became qualified to work with prisoners. I make my living primarily in executive assessment and development. So, the answer turns out to be a joke that needs no punch line: I learned how to work with criminals by working with executives.

Seriously, there are parallels. One similarity is that—based on our personality types—there are certain words that have more of an emotional charge. While trigger words such as fairness, trust and authenticity, for example, have some emotional weight for all of us, each of us has at least one such word that really gets us juiced. One guesses the juiciness of our trigger word comes from not getting enough of what the word represents.

Inmates in my program seem easily distracted. Part of the problem is that, for safety, the classroom we work in is windows on three sides. Guards and other inmates are constantly walking by and talking. Nonetheless, starting my recent class, I wanted to improve the on-task time individually and collectively. I came up with the phrase, "Respect the Man" as a reminder to stop side activities and pay attention to whomever was talking.

This entreaty has taken off. Now, I am not the only one using the phrase. They even say it to me!

I can't help but conclude the word "respect" has a special emotional charge in prison, probably because there is such a short supply.

## A Fellow Alum in Prison
### (POSTED 13 SEPTEMBER 2018)

Striking to me in my work in prison is how much the inmates have in common with the rest of us. We like to think of the inmates as very, very "other." However, they talk about their families, they talk about sports and politics just like the rest of us.

Clearly, each of them has done something very bad. They are all felons. But no one is completely bad and no one is completely good. They all were someone's baby at one time.

An inmate named Terry brought this home to me. He talked about his background and I found he attended the same grade school as I, St. Vivian's in Finneytown, a nice middle-class neighborhood in Cincinnati.

## You Can't Judge a Prison by its Cover
### (POSTED 18 FEBRUARY 2018)

Lebanon Correctional—where I have been volunteering for some time—is a Level 3 & 4 prison; 4 is maximum security. This week, I moved to a Level 1 facility, Warren Correctional, which is a reintegration unit for those within a year or two of being released.

Used to Level 4 security, I entered the Warren Correctional lobby and noticed a prisoner not quite in the lobby and out of the view of the guard who was checking me in. The prisoner was a big man and looked like he could be the lead singer in a heavy metal band.

Before this, the only prisoner I saw in a prison lobby was in chains and hand cuffs with a guard on each side. So, I studied the guard to see if he knew the prisoner was there. I could not tell. The guard finished my processing and I sat on the lobby bench.

The prisoner comes over and sits next to me, smiles, holds out his hand, introduces himself, telling me he was going to be in my group and was looking forward to it. Later, in our session, he stepped into the role of Sargeant-at-Arms, getting chairs, rounding up the other inmates, etc.

## Inside Job in Prison
### (POSTED 12 JANUARY 2019)

A handful of inmates at Lebanon Correctional Institute work in the Tag Shop making and distributing "Specialized Interest" Ohio license plates. One was grinning like the Cheshire Cat when he came into my classroom this Wednesday. He asked, "Did you get your tags?" Here's the background.

During the prior week, on Monday, I ordered FCCincinnati "Specialized Interest" plates. The clerk gave me a 30-day temporary tag and said that often the plates take more than a month to get mailed. She said I could contact her if I did not have them by month's end.

Two days later, I inquired of my Tag Shop inmates if the FCCincinnati plates would have the new Major League Soccer logo. In the discussion,

I said that I had ordered the tags two days earlier.

Three days after that discussion, Saturday, the FCCincinnati tags showed up in my mail box. So much for waiting a month or more; I got mine in six days. Knowing only my first name, the grinning inmate said that when the orders arrived there was only one Tom getting FCCincinnati plates.

## Being the Bad Guy in Prison
### (POSTED 13 APRIL 2019)

In our Catholic Studies prison sessions, we divide the inmates into four groups of about 15, each group with a set classroom. Every nine weeks, we volunteers rotate classrooms to a new group.

The group I just finished has been found difficult to manage and keep on topic by all of the volunteers. My last nine weeks was no exception. Presumably, inmates are in our program to learn, or at least listen, and I have only one rule, "Respect The Man," meaning not interrupting or side-talking.

Two in this difficult group have had the hardest time following the rule. Clearly, they are not there to learn. This week, I could not get them to cooperate. My efforts to get them to cooperate led to them challenging me, for example, one saying I was "lying" and the other gratuitously saying "prove it" when I said something that was patently true.

One asserted that I did not care about him to which I replied, "I'm here."

Then, as often happens in group dynamics, otherwise constructive inmates began piling on. There was more side talking, interrupting, and giving me grief.

When I got home I emailed the Director of Prison Ministries requesting that the two be removed from the program. She did so.

## I Must Be Getting Used to Prison
### (POSTED 13 APRIL 2019)

I've been volunteering in prison since June of 2016. This week, waiting for the inmates to trickle into my classroom, I chatted with the few who had already arrived. Commonly, inmates whom I have worked with but are not currently in my group come in to say hello.

I sat with my back to the door and I felt hands on my shoulders in what I regarded as a friendly gesture. Not being able to see whose hands were laid upon me, I said lightly, "Who's back there?" The visitor, on his way to another group, was an inmate whom I have known from the start. We exchanged pleasantries and he left for his classroom.

Driving home and reflecting on the session, I remembered that my visitor had disclosed that he is from out of state and came to Ohio only to murder someone whom he also dismembered in a bathtub. While the thought of such a person's hands on my shoulders should, perhaps, have been chilling, I was nonetheless not bothered. It is hard to demonize people whom you come to know.

# CHAPTER 2

# How Prison Works: Toilet Training in Prison

*You have to learn the rules of the game.*
*And then, you have to play better than anyone else.*
ALBERT EINSTEIN

Prisons have their own problems and, therefore, their own rules. Some of the common practices seem quite weird until one thinks about their context. Safety and security beat out all other concerns in prison. Hard decisions have to be made quickly. Inmates have to learn to get along.

### Toilet Training in Prison
### (POSTED 15 JUNE 2017)

At Lebanon Correctional, two inmates share a 6 by 8-foot cell. There is a bunk bed and a stainless-steel toilet-sink combo. I understand the toilet-sink combo to be a small version of a toilet with a sink as if it were on top of the toilet tank. Also, the toilet seat is built-in, is part of the toilet, and is not hinged. You can't lift up the toilet seat.

You can find one online. Only $3,239.00. Suicide resistant!

Inmates have explained how cellmates, or "cellies," as they call them, have to come to terms on the use of the toilet. First off, without a hinged toilet seat, there at the least has to be an understanding on one's cleaning responsibility after a standing micturation. Another issue is that the toilets can be flushed only once every 6 minutes. Flush sooner than 6 minutes and the toilet will not be flushable again for an hour.

Not surprisingly, toilet training one's cellie is often a topic of complaint.

### A Forty-Three Percent Pay Increase in Prison
### (POSTED 14 OCTOBER 2016)

I asked an inmate, Francis, about jobs he had while in prison. All inmates have jobs, all seem to want to have jobs, and some jobs are better than others. He started in the kitchen where he earned $35 a month for a 40-hour workweek. (I learned that inmates who work in the kitchen may get second servings. In fact, he gained 32 pounds!)

Specialized Interest, Ohio license plates are made by inmates at Lebanon and those jobs pay better. Moving to the "Tag Shop" from the kitchen, Francis raised his income 43% to $50 a month. He expressed an ambition to get promoted and eventually earn the top wage, $80 a month.

Bob, another inmate who already is at top pay in the Lebanon Tag Shop just had his annual security review and is being promoted to Chillicothe, a Level 1 & 2 prison. Chillicothe makes standard Ohio license plates in two shops. One, however, has more overtime and Bob is trying to get assigned there.

### Eight Days in the Hole
#### (POSTED 12 NOVEMBER 2016)

One of the inmates at Lebanon Correctional is captain of his prison track team. I call him "Reverend" because of his ability to quote the Bible. A volunteer comes in on some weekends and trains and coaches them.

Reverend has that lean distance-runner build and tries to train every-day as an example to his teammates. Looking at Lebanon Correctional on a map with satellite view, one can see the "yard" with a worn path near the outer edge where inmates can run.

During the day, various inmates may be in the yard. Recently, while Reverend was on the path running, a fight broke out between rival groups in the yard. He said guards came running from everywhere to stop the fight.

Unfortunately, he was running near the fight and looked to a guard as if he were running from having fought so as not to get caught. He got nabbed, was required to lie prone, and was handcuffed. Like those who were fighting, he was put in "the hole," solitary confinement.

Luckily there are cameras in the yard. Unluckily, eight days was required to establish his non-involvement.

## Couuuunnt Tiiime in Prison
### (POSTED 18 MAY 2017)

Seems like every week in prison I learn about some rule or activity I never even imagined existed. This week, my surprise was count time or "couuuunnt tiiime" as the inmates say when imitating the guards' announcement.

Safety and security is always paramount. Thus, count time is a common practice in prisons—four times a day. If not at the work locations, prisoners have to be in their cells. Prisoners can find having to rush to their cells to be counted and waiting until the count is finished demeaning.

Lebanon Correctional's 4:15 PM count time last night brought counting to my attention. We start at 5:00 PM and inmates are immediately filing in from various cell blocks, passes in hand to show to our Correction Officer. Yesterday, they did not come right away. The Catholic Ministries Director said, "They must not have cleared the 4:15 count." Clearing count means that every one of the 2,500 inmates has been accounted for, having been counted by hand.

Eventually they started to come. I have to document my group's attendance by having them sign a form. At the top of the form is a spot for me to put the date, my name and the number of inmates. I used to visibly count heads—just like the Corrections Officers. Last night I adopted a new practice of covert counting.

## Memorial Day Ceremony in Prison
### (POSTED 26 MAY 2017)

During my normal chatting with my Prison Response-Ability inmates at Lebanon Correctional this week, I learned that inmates who are military veterans stage a Memorial Day Ceremony. Also, in the run-up to the day, they fund raise!

One fund raiser, to my surprise, is a bake sale. The vets with the help of prison staff get a donut maker to deliver donuts. Inmates order donuts—a real treat in prison—and pay through their prison accounts. (Signs near the entrance remind those entering prison that along with the obvious prohibition on guns, cell phones and drugs, cash is prohibited on the property.) There is also a fun run in the yard with a $3 entry fee. The guards can participate, too.

Ohio Military Veterans in prison get their dues paid by the Veterans Association. The ceremony includes the reading of names of Ohioans KIA and MIA. Crosses are placed on the grounds of the ceremony with the numbers lost in wars back to the Civil War.

So, what happens to the funds? They are donated to charity, primarily the Special Olympics. How much? $150,000 over the last ten years.

### Checking in to the Hole
(POSTED 24 AUGUST 2017)

You might call my current 8-week session a 201 level course. As a prerequisite to attend, an inmate must have completed my original 101 course. This allowed me some leeway to choose more committed students.

This Wednesday night was week 7 and, while an inmate missing a single session is not unusual, I had one who did not show up for a third week. So, I inquired and was surprised to learn that he has been in solitary confinement—the hole—for three weeks! The other inmates told me he "checked in." They explained that you can ask to be put in the hole.

Why would you do so? Protection.

Inmates barter with and buy from each other—yes, apparently even drugs—and some "creditor" inmates will get violent over unpaid debts. Problem is the guards will interrogate inmates checking in to the hole to find out who might be selling drugs. Snitching is even more likely to result in violence than unpaid drug debts.

### Unwelcome Visitors in Prison
(POSTED 28 SEPTEMBER 2017)

At Lebanon Correctional in the Prison Response-Ability Project, we start every Wednesday night at 5:00 PM. Normally, we just chat for the first fifteen minutes, waiting for everyone to arrive. Somehow, this week, we got on the subject of roaches.

The inmates' discussion made clear that roaches can be common in some cells. They can be more or less plentiful depending on the sanitation habits of cellblock neighbors. Wanting to get a sense of how many roaches, I conducted a survey. I asked, "First thing in the morning, how many roaches do you typically have to kill?" Answers ranged from 3-4 to 9-10 each morning in a 6 by 8-foot cell.

So, then, inmates shared advice on dealing with roaches. Their approaches range from mixing a poison made from toothpaste and industrial soap powder, to catching one of the frogs often present in the prison yard where they exercise and keeping the insectivore in one's cell. Stories of pet frogs kept for as long as a year in a cell followed.

### "Establishing" in Prison
(POSTED 3 AUGUST 2018)

I remember reading about Nelson Mandela's development of warm relationships with his prison guards despite laboring under hard conditions. Such "establishing," as this is called at Lebanon Correctional, is prohibited: Rule (24) Establishing or attempting to establish a personal relationship with an employee...contractor...volunteer...

During Session 3 of the Prison Responsibility Project this week, this topic came up. While at first this rule seems unnecessarily unkind—and certainly not designed to foster rehabilitation—it makes sense.

For example, upon establishing a relationship with a guard, employee, or volunteer, inmates may try to have a relative or friend contact the person, even offering money, to smuggle something in or perform an illicit favor.

Because of Rule 24, inmates are not supposed to ask—and we volunteers should not respond to too many—questions about our personal lives.

### Being on Guard in Prison
(POSTED 3 MAY 2018)

Prison guards, properly known as Corrections Officers, have a tough job. This week, I had time to chat with one of the guards in the lobby and also with the guard escorting us to the education room, known as our "ride."

As background, Lebanon Correctional holds about 2,500 inmates and has a staff of about 500 with some 330 being guards. So, if you do the math, overall the prisoners outnumber the guards 7 to 1. But, if you add the time dimension of 24-hours-a-day coverage, 21 to 1 becomes the ratio.

Guards have to be constantly on guard not just because they are outnumbered. I learned that guards suffer inmate assaults an average of three times in a career.

The young guard I was talking to had already been assaulted three times. He described one incident as typical, saying that he caught an inmate with contraband and his effort to take it from the inmate resulted in him being assaulted.

The other guard reminded me that Lebanon houses convicted murderers and, he said currently, a serial killer. Also, his experience has been that a normally compliant inmate can suddenly act out due to any number of things, especially bad news from home.

### Locked Out of Prison
(POSTED 27 APRIL 2018)

I followed my normal routine this week, leaving in the late afternoon for Lebanon Correctional. But, rarely is there a normal routine in prison work.

This week, we did not get past the ID check. The Corrections Officer at the lobby control desk advised, "Sorry, we're shut down." Naturally, one of the volunteers asked, "Why?" But the only answer the CO could offer was the same, "We're shut down. No one in or out."

Worst case scenario would be gang violence. Best case would be just a failure to clear the 4:15 PM prisoner count.

The following week we learned the problem had been gang violence and the mood after a week of heavy restrictions was quite subdued. The inmates were not themselves, somewhat robotic.

### 2.4 Cubic Feet in Prison
(POSTED 26 FEBRUARY 2018)

The inmates at the Lebanon Level 1 unit in my Prison Response-Ability Project don't have many personal belongings. In last week's discussion, I learned they are subject to quarterly "2.4 cubic feet personal belongings inspections."

Here's how these inspections work. For the daily counts, inmates must all go to and remain at their respective cubicles until the count is completed. The 2.4 inspections are added to one of the counts. Each inmate must fit his total personal belongings into a 2.4 cubic foot space. Anything that does not fit must be gotten rid of. State issued clothing is not included, but personal clothing such as tee shirts are, including shoes. (We had a good laugh about one of my inmates with size 15 shoes.)

If you want to see how many of your belongings can be placed within a 2.4 cubic foot space, just get a box that is about 20 inches by 20 inches by 10 inches and give it a try.

## Turning 6 Months into 6 Years in Prison
### (POSTED 7 MARCH 2019)

How inmates react to guards and authority figures can mean a world of difference. Controlling reactivity is something we spend a great deal of time on. Two contrasting examples showed up in one session.

One inmate, James, explained how he turned a six months sentence into a six-year sentence. The discussion was occasioned, in stark contrast, by my congratulating Ralph, another inmate as he came into class late.

About ten minutes before Ralph entered class, I watched a guard stop him for wearing the wrong shirt for our location. (An inmate can be in a white tee shirt on the block, but must be wearing a blue collared shirt in the cafeteria, education rooms, etc.) Watching him and the guard, I wasn't so sure Ralph was going to remain respectful. He did and I complimented him when he eventually returned.

This resulted in James relating how early in his 6-month sentence he assaulted six different guards, including breaking a nose and an eye socket. He knew there would be some consequences, but he said it got his attention when he landed back in court, charged with multiple assaults, and ended up with a six-year sentence.

## From Prison to Emergency Room
### (POSTED 5 APRIL 2019)

During the Prison Response-Ability Program sessions at Lebanon Correctional, I am always inquiring of the inmates how otherwise normal activities are handled in prison. One inmate told the story of needing medical attention.

He burned himself with boiling water while making coffee in his cell one night. Come morning, the prison medical staff determined he needed to be taken to an emergency room. OSU hospital has facilities to handle the incarcerated. He described holding cells for inmates in the basement of the Columbus, Ohio facility.

To get from Lebanon to OSU requires a van and two guards. The van has a caged area in the back for inmates. In addition, inmates are shackled to the cage. So, getting someone out requires two steps, unlocking the cage and unlocking the shackles.

This description released a flurry of inmate stories how such prison transports became involved in accidents, including one where two female inmates died in a fiery crash, unable to be rescued.

## Your Prison Vocabulary Builder
### (POSTED 17 MARCH 2017)

The inmates at Lebanon Correctional in my Prison Response-Ability Project have their own vocabulary for many things.

**There are vocabulary words for people:**

Cellie – Cellmate

Grey Shirt – Correctional Officer

White Shirt – Ranking Correctional Supervisor (lieutenants and captains with officer bars on their collars)

**There are vocabulary words for items:**

Mush Fake – Fabricating something from existing material

Shank – Homemade knife

Commissary – Any item purchased from the inmate store

State Blues – State issued clothing

**Places:**

Cell Block – Living area with two-man cells

Day Room – Limited access open living area on the first floor of each cell block

Hole – Jail for offenders who do not follow the rules

**Activities:**

Check In – Request for placement in protective custody

Get Paid – Paroled

Flop – Get denied parole

Shakedown – Search, typically, person or cell

Six Five – Warning that an Officer is coming

Crash – Start a fight in front of a Correctional Officer to get someone else (and yourself) thrown into the Hole

# CHAPTER 3

# Humor: Prison, A Gated Community

*A good friend will bail you out of jail. A true friend will be sitting next to you saying, "Damn, we screwed up!"*

UNKNOWN

I have not had anyone tell a joke in prison, but, mostly good-natured ribbing is common. Nonetheless, I've never seen any inmate break loose in full-bodied laughter. Being inconspicuous is safer. Acting big can draw the attention of guards and bullies.

In these posts, you will see, we had some good—if restrained—laughs.

## A Funny Thing Happened in Prison the Other Day
### (POSTED 5 JULY 2016)

We start our prison sessions by acknowledging birthdays for the week. The birthday celebrating inmate is asked where he wants to go on his birthday free day (don't worry, it's completely imaginary) and what meal he will have. An inmate with a sense of humor said his preferred destination was, "Any country without a US extradition treaty." For his meal, "Anything not prepared by Aramark."

A second inmate was more typical simply wishing to see his family and go to Wendy's.

## Prison, a Gated Community
### (POSTED 4 DECEMBER 2017)

Every Wednesday, when I am delivering the Prison Response-Ability Project course, the difference between my life style and the inmates' is painfully obvious. Sometimes, I come right from work in full regalia: nice suit, silk tie, tailored shirt, etc. Their prison-issue clothing, not stylish to begin with, must receive pretty rough treatment in the laundry and elsewhere. They often comment on my clothes, shoes, watches, etc.

They will also ask about cars and other status related items.

I always try to play down the differences. On a recent night, one of them offered me some of his candy and I declined saying he needed it more than me. This triggered a round of mocking comments about me being able to get anything I want when they can't.

I thought the time was right for me to have some fun too. I said, "Wait, wait, wait, where I come from, you guys are the wealthy ones." That got their attention and raised their curiosity. I pointed out that to get into their neighborhood every week I have to get past their guard gate. Their guard checks my ID to see if I am on their VIP list. I said, "Where I come from, gated communities are where rich people live. You live in the most guarded and gated community I've ever been allowed into."

## The Black Prisoner Named Scott
### (POSTED 18 SEPTEMBER 2016)

When we started my current group of Prison Responsibility Project inmates at Lebanon Correctional, we did the normal introductions, first name only. One of the black inmates introducing himself as Scott said, "I'll bet I'm the only black guy you ever met named Scott." After thinking for a moment, I told him he was right.

My grandchildren are black, so I then said, "I'll bet you've never seen anyone who looked like me with two black grandchildren." He said, "I've never seen anyone who looked like you in my neighborhood, period."

## No Complaints in Prison
### (POSTED 9 JUNE 2017)

A key basis for self-response-ability in the Prison Response-Ability Project is self-awareness. The notion is simple, we cannot change that of which we are unaware. Or, quoting the famous Swiss psychiatrist Carl Jung, "Until you make the unconscious conscious, it will direct your life and you will call it fate."

Always looking for awareness triggers that I can teach my inmates, I came across Complaint Free World rubber bracelets. The idea is to wear a Complaint Free bracelet to remind yourself not to complain. You might be surprised how much time we waste complaining. (Confronting someone with whom you have an issue is not complaining. Carping about someone else is complaining.)

My PRP inmates saw my bracelet, asked me about the approach, and wanted to try. I got them bracelets and coached them on noticing how unconsciously their complaints arise. I explained my experience that I noticed how my complaints were out of my mouth before I even realized. There was no real thought; to me, they arose unconsciously. Thus, they became great awareness triggers.

Complaining is pandemic in prison. My inmates, understandably, had mixed results. On the humorous side, one said he made it nine hours, adding, "And, then I woke up." Another said he made it all week. So, I asked, "How do you like the food here?" He wisely did not answer. A few have stayed with the program and I can see their progress.

### ROTFL in Prison
#### (POSTED 26 NOVEMBER 2018)

One night when I got home from offering the Prison Response-Ability Project session at Lebanon Correctional, I related a funny incident from that night to Mrs. Hattersley. The story was one of those You-Had-To-Be-There types and not that funny in the retelling. But, at the time, I busted out a belly laugh that qualified for "Rolling On The Floor Laughing."

She asked, how did the inmates react. I stopped and was surprised to realize that I have never in the years of working in prison seen one of the inmates bust a gut laughing. Yes, they will chuckle, but there is always a deadening sense of keeping their feelings hidden.

# CHAPTER 4

# Food: The Joy of Cooking in Prison

*Man shall not live by bread alone,*
*except a man who has no bread.*

UNKNOWN

Not surprisingly, food is very important to the inmates mainly because there is so little else to look forward to. Nonetheless, complaining about the food is standard fare. In these posts, food and drink play a central role, but not always for consumption.

## The Joy of Cooking in Prison
### (POSTED 5 JULY 2016)

At Lebanon, cafeteria food is not well liked. (The inmates would use stronger language.) And, second servings are not permitted. (Unless you work in the kitchen.) So, every two weeks when the prison store is open, getting food is important. And, inmates can have crockpot cookers in their cells.

This week before the start of my Prison Responsibility Project session, one of the inmates and I started talking and our discussion somehow went to food. So, of course, we shared recipes! Well actually, I was very interested to learn how many dishes can be cooked in a crockpot and, as I learned, even a broken crockpot can be useful.

So, here's a recipe for you.

Take a bag of potato chips and crumble them into an aluminum pie pan that you saved from the pie you purchased at the prison commissary.

Put in small amounts of hot water from your new crockpot until the crumbled chips have a consistency similar to hash browns.

Spread the potato chip-hash brown dough onto the inside of the flattened potato chip bag you saved to a thickness between ¼ and ½ inch. Reusing the bag keeps your cell clean and the oil already on the bag prevents sticking.

Cut the dough into bread-slice sizes with something other than a knife.

At the same time, heat the oil you saved from the canned salmon or tuna fish in the pie pan you saved from the commissary pie with the heating element you saved when your old crockpot broke.

Cook your potato chip-hash browns in the pie pan until golden brown. Serve your transformed potato chips warm.

Bon appetite.

## Mac & Cheese in Prison
### (POSTED 5 JULY 2016)

Visitors are not allowed to bring food in for inmates. However, inmates do earn a small amount of money and visitors can put money in spending accounts for them. Every two weeks, inmates have access to the prison store to buy food. Kraft Macaroni & Cheese Dinner is a favorite and can be cooked in a cell if an inmate owns a crockpot.

One of my inmates, Steve, has been imprisoned for decades. Two weeks ago, we were talking about anger and Steve told a story about his new cellmate who is unused to the ways of prison. The new guy annoys Steve at about every turn.

Steve related that the new cellie wanted to prepare Mac & Cheese using Steve's crockpot. He gave his new cellie step-by-step instructions. Heat the water first, etc. Nonetheless, the cellie just put everything in at once and turned on the heat. The result was an inedible, glutinous glob.

Steve became enraged and threw the Mac & Cheese at the cell wall. Given Steve's size and appearance, the cellie is likely smaller, quieter and not half as mean looking. He had to fear for his safety.

Then, last week we were talking about shame. Steve spoke up about the Mac & Cheese incident he had related the week before. He said that after telling the story at our meeting he was so ashamed of his anger that he could not sleep and he awakened his cellie at 2:00 AM to apologize. (Probably, at first, giving him another good scare.)

## Chipotle in Prison
### (POSTED 5 JULY 2016)

We had our Christmas party last week, and were able to bring food in from the outside. I saw how the simple things in life can mean so much: soda pop, Ritz crackers, tortilla chips, cookies, brownies, etc. I had to explain to one inmate what the gooey green stuff was. Calling it guacamole was inadequate; I had to back up and talk about avocados.

One inmate named Alex in particular made me reflect. He had never eaten a Chipotle Burrito before. He savored that burrito like he was tasting fine wine. Alex is 61 years old, was incarcerated in 1983, and is getting out soon. 1983...Ronald Reagan, Michael Jackson's "Thriller," and the Dow Jones at 1100. No minivan, no internet, no cell phone, and no Chipotle.

Once we ate, we sang Christmas carols. After, "God Rest Ye Merry Gentlemen," an inmate went around the room asking the others what they were "Merry" for. Some needed time to think, but the Chipotle savoring Alex said right away, "I am merry because I am alive and I am not angry the way I used to be."

## Making Wine in Prison
### (POSTED 5 JULY 2016)

We start sessions at Lebanon Correctional with me asking for news anyone wants to share, inviting especially good news. One inmate who is three months from being released related he is on thirty days of restrictions: took his TV, can't use the prison phone, can't download emails, limited commissary visits, and no visitors.

Why? He got caught with five gallons of prison wine.

I learned that prison wine requires a starter solution which can be easily created by fermenting fruit juice. Add one gallon of water, a pound of sugary candy, and a bottle of ketchup. (Yes, ketchup.) Mix all this up in a properly ventilated garbage bag and in merely days you get wine.

Going price...$25 a gallon.

## Tough Love in Prison
### (POSTED 5 JULY 2016)

My project is under the supervision of the Director of Prison Ministries for the Catholic Archdiocese of Cincinnati. Each week, she provides a small bag of candy for each attending inmate.

Even cheap candy is very important to the inmates and the sweeter, the better. In the Director's absence, I once brought trail mix in instead. Forget it. I have never gotten so much grief. Since attendance varies for a laundry list of reasons, we sometimes have more candy than inmates. The extras are highly coveted and usually divvied up.

I delegate candy management to an inmate. This week my candy man passed out the candy, kept the extras, told me he had a law library pass (for which inmates are allowed to leave early), and left with four bags of candy.

The Director is not easily fooled. She caught on, had his cell searched, and by the time we left he was in the hole—solitary confinement. Just bags of candy, but stealing nonetheless.

## 18 Days of Bacon in Prison
### (POSTED 5 JULY 2016)

One of my inmates named Anthony was hospitalized for eighteen days at OSU hospital. Inmates habitually complain about the food in prison, blaming and defaming their food service company, Aramark.

When he got to OSU, he was delighted to learn that he could actually order food there, i.e., choose from a menu. To his surprise, he could even order bacon for breakfast. Pork is not served in prison, presumably, to avoid any religious food taboos.

To him, the food was gourmet compared to prison food. Anthony said he ordered bacon the first day and every day during his eighteen-day hospital stay.

His delight prompted him to ask who the food service provider was. And he still can't believe what they told him. The food service company at OSU hospital is also Aramark.

# CHAPTER 5

# Family: Three Sisters in Prison

*All happy families are alike;*
*each unhappy family is unhappy in its own way.*
TOLSTOY

This chapter's topic is family which is a much more common topic among inmates than I expected. Nonetheless, as Tolstoy warned in the quote above, expect the unexpected with prison families.

## Three Sisters in Prison
### (POSTED 6 JANUARY 2018)

At Lebanon Correctional, our current Prison Responsibility Project class will be complete next week. I advised them that I won't be back for a while because I am going to present my classes at Dayton Correctional, a women's prison. Quickly, one said, "Make sure my sister gets in your class. She's there." I started to think what a coincidence when another said, "Darn, my sister was there, but got moved." Then a third topped it off saying, "I'm glad my sister has gotten out now."

## "It's a Wonderful Life" in Prison
### (POSTED 18 JANUARY 2019)

This week, the inmates were to have journaled on the following:

*What is Interconnectedness? Martin Luther King Jr. described inter-connectedness as being "caught in an inescapable network of mutu-ality, tied together into a single garment of destiny." The movie "It's a Wonderful Life," in which an angel shows a frustrated businessman what the world would have been like if he had not existed, captured this truth in such a moving story that it became a classic.*

*If I had never existed...*

27

Not surprisingly, many answers were negative but true, such as, "Fewer people would have been using drugs." "My victim would be alive." "My family would not have had to deal with me and my problems."

A couple tended towards nihilism, "nothing would be different." Nonetheless, by my probing about their families, especially about children, they opened up to the positive. Most had at least a set of grandparents, children, or someone whose lives they could say would have been less without them.

### "What Do I Value?" in Prison
#### (POSTED 6 DECEMBER 2018)

Every week, we review the inmates' journaling assignment. This week the topic was, "What do I value?"

There were commonalities and outliers. Most common were "Respect, Loyalty, Integrity, and Honesty." Somewhat common were "Family and Friends." Outliers were "Alone Time and Life."

### What People in Prison Think About
#### (POSTED 13 JULY 2018)

Starting a new session, one of my repeat attenders, Jimmy, whom I had not talked to for a while updated me, telling me he had only a year left on his three-year sentence. I asked him his plans.

Top of mind for him and, encouragingly, for many of the inmates, is getting his life together so he could see his children, three sons with the oldest age 11. The prison library has legal resources and he has already prepared and printed the motions he is going to file when freed for visitation and custody rights to be with his sons.

### Sibling Rivalry in Prison
#### (POSTED 11 MAY 2018)

I have an inmate named Angel who has been incarcerated for 28 years and, with gratitude, relates that his parents have supported him the whole time. Including with money.

Our discussion this week covered the heart as a center of intelligence and self-awareness. This triggered Angel to relate a heartfelt, family story.

He explained that he got his brother's mail by mistake. (I was puzzled.) Turns out, his brother is in a lower level correctional facility on the same campus. The letter was from their parents. So, he opened the envelope.

Unfortunately, by opening the letter, he learned that his parents were regularly sending more money to his brother than to him.

## How to Avoid Prison Time
### (POSTED 7 APRIL 2018)

This week in prison, dealing with families kept coming up. Not surprisingly, prison—and crime—can create difficult family issues.

Effective prosecutorial work includes getting co-defendants to testify against one another. The testifier pleads to a lesser offense and stays out of prison. One of my inmate's drug enterprise included his son, a young man not old enough to buy alcohol. The son—with his father's encouragement—testified against his father to avoid prison.

The son, the father reports, quit his job and left the relationship with the mother of his children on the day he testified against his father. The young man has fallen into depression and substance abuse and has been taken in by his grandparents.

## The "Worry Box" in Prison
### (POSTED 7 APRIL 2017)

At my session this week, all of the inmates cited wanting to see their families—mainly their children—first thing when they get out. This turned the discussion to dealing with family issues while in prison.

Inmates have controlled access to telephones and email, enabling them to stay in touch. But the telephone is called "The Worry Box" by one of them. He said, and others agreed, that not being able to deal with family problems is one of the most difficult limitations in prison. They pointed out that some inmates drive themselves crazy by still trying to run their families' lives while in prison.

# CHAPTER 6

# Surprises: How I Met
# My Father...in Prison

*Let us accept truth, even when it surprises us and alters our views.*
GEORGE SAND

Prison is sad, but sometimes the sadness jumps out of the darkness and nearly strangles you. Thankfully, there are good surprises, too.

## How I Met my Father...in Prison
### (POSTED 20 JULY 2017)

I was told a story about two inmates that I just can't quit thinking about.

The older of the two inmates was and still is incarcerated at Lebanon Correctional. He told the story about another, younger inmate arriving at Lebanon who had never met his father. The father had left the family while the younger inmate was an infant and they never saw each other again.

Never saw each other again, that is, until the younger inmate whose name was Paul Jefferson met the older inmate whose name was Paul Jefferson.

They were father and son.

## I Hate This Prison...Don't Make Me Leave
### (POSTED 1 SEPTEMBER 2016)

One week we worked on understanding anger, talking about experiencing anger with an open heart and mind. Many of us were socialized to feel guilty about our anger, but that teaching is wrong. Anger is a normal, highly adaptive feeling that is telling us that something is wrong, a form of intelligence. How we deal with that feeling needs to be socialized, not whether we experience the feeling.

So, we worked with the inmates on recognizing their anger, taking responsibility for their anger, and experiencing anger in a healthy way. To do so, each was asked to take a moment to sense what he felt angry about right then.

An inmate named Bob had been cleared to move to a less restrictive prison. He was the first to speak up about his anger. We wondered, what did he have to be angry about?

Friendship is especially important to him and he had to choose between more freedom at Level 2 and his friends at Level 3 & 4. He felt anger at being forced to give up his friends.

## The Scariest Thing in Prison
### (POSTED 16 DECEMBER 2016)

We had a speaker this week for the whole Catholic studies group. He was incarcerated for 12 years, has been out 8, and has a family. He works for St Vincent DePaul helping other returning citizens transition.

While we were waiting for him to start, I sat amongst the inmates. The one on my left told me he was soon being moved to a lower level prison to get better care for his Parkinson's, diabetes and other health issues. He said he had never been more worried about anything in his life than how he would be able to handle the transition.

The one who was on my right is about to be released. He has a terrible addiction problem and, while he wants to go to his hometown to be with his children, he is extremely worried about being back in the old environment that supported his addiction.

The speaker was impressive. Mid-forties, tall, athletic, well-spoken, family-man, but truly straight out of Compton. He came to Ohio from California to sell drugs and ended up convicted of armed robbery and involuntary manslaughter in a drug deal gone bad. (I don't think there is such a thing as a drug deal gone good.)

I saw many a head nod when he said to the group that for him the scariest part of prison was getting out!

## Soccer and Sanity in Prison
### (POSTED 28 OCTOBER 2018)

The inmates often mention their visits to "mental health." Good to know help is available, but I often wonder whether more help should be made available.

The inmates journal every week. This eight-week session, their assigned, weekly journal questions come from the book, SQ21, *The Twenty-One Skills of Spiritual Intelligence*. For the question, "What is my life's purpose?" one inmate said his was to help the US Men's National Soccer Team win the World Cup and, thereby, bring about world peace.

I've never been around such a clear expression of dissociative disorder and wonder whether he needs more than a general population prison can provide.

His speech is generally rambling and hard to follow. I've been trying to figure out how to reach him. Quick research on dissociative disorder showed the top two risks as suicide and self-harm.

## DIY in Prison
### (POSTED 3 MARCH 2017)

No one would be surprised to learn that Lebanon Correctional is—I don't mean to be unkind here—not well decorated. In fact, the colors, if not white, are one of fifty shades of grey.

I was told by one of my inmates that the cell walls are painted all white. He has an artistic streak and decided his cell needed a makeover. Like anyone doing a makeover with limited resources, he had to be imaginative.

Since anything that is not painted white is painted grey, his color palette was thusly limited. There are no prison paint stores, so he had to get paint from maintenance workers, most of whom are fellow prisoners. Same thing getting a paint brush.

So, somehow—I told him I did not want to know how—he got grey paint and a brush to his cell. First, he added what sounds like a grey wainscot. That needed to be complemented with a grey crown molding. Apparently having created a too predictable, symmetrical look, he painted what he called an old-fashioned, crooked, grey border around his mirror.

The Correctional Officers for his cell block liked his work such that he was asked if he would do some decorative painting in their office.

## Managing Workers in Prison
### (POSTED 9 JANUARY 2019)

My career has been in Human Resources and I've counseled countless leaders on employee problems. One inmate named Roger, whom I have known since I started the project a few years ago, is a leadman in the Tag Shop. He has three people under his supervision. Apparently, like most of us, during his free time Roger thinks about work.

I am often surprised how inmates think and talk about the same things we all do; families, politics, sports, etc. But this was the first time I gave away free consulting. Roger started questioning me about how to better manage a problem employee. The problem he described, the way he described the problem, and how much he cared about finding the right solution reminded me of countless conversations I had with ambitious entrepreneurs and executives over the years.

## Here Comes Revenge, Here Comes Prison
### (POSTED 28 JULY 2017)

I think I know what Lars Ulrich and James Alan Hetfield of Metallica were thinking when they wrote "Here Comes Revenge." Particularly the line, "Countless hatreds built my shrine, I was born in anger's flame."

My inmates have a journaling assignment due every week when we meet on Wednesday evenings. This week's started with the instruction, "Recall an unsettling or sad event." Three more instructions followed about how to process the feelings that arose around the event.

How unsettling and sad their events were was striking. I had a social worker as a guest. Even she—despite her experience with others' difficulties—was visibly moved by what she heard.

One is a story of Tony and how revenge landed him in prison. The sad event started with the memory of his mother dropping him off in foster care around age nine, saying, "I can't handle him." Tony summarized his experience in foster care describing the foster parents as just wanting the paycheck.

At eighteen and on his own, he was hired by a moving company. Having anger still obvious today, he smiled when he described his revenge—even though it landed him in prison. Tony took a van and completely emptied both households, his mother's and his foster parents.

## CHAPTER 7

# Progress: Having a Proud Pee in Prison

*The truest help we can render an afflicted man
is not to take his burden from him,
but to call out his best energy,
that he may be able to bear the burden.*

PHILLIPS BROOKS

While I find prison work fulfilling, I do not always find it easy. However, when those occasional break-throughs occur like the sun bursting through on a cloudy day, I am re-energized.

You will read about some of the best moments I've had in prison in this chapter.

### Having A Proud Pee in Prison
#### (POSTED 8 SEPTEMBER 2017)

Our work this week focused on understanding that the feelings associated with our heart are forms of intelligence. Our shame, sadness, envy and pride are to be acknowledged as telling us something important.

So, we took a couple of minutes for silent meditation to sense the feelings of our hearts. I went around the room asking the inmates what came up for them. An inmate named Wayne, "pride."

He explained that he was pulled out of bed at 6:30 AM for a drug screen. Not randomly, remember prisoners do not have the full rights of citizenship. Inmates can be tested on mere suspicion.

He felt pride, sensing the nervousness of the other inmates waiting their turns. He had been a user in the past—yes, while in prison—and had succeeded in becoming clean. Wayne was looking forward to proving his success.

## Appreciation in Prison
(POSTED 28 JULY 2016)

We cover Dr. David Daniels' Universal Growth Process, also known as the Five A's of Transformation: Awareness, Acceptance, Appreciation, Action, and Adherence. This week we covered Appreciation.

More than a little worry came up for me when I had to utter Dr. Daniels' words, "Appreciation is manifesting gratitude for the positives in life." I was ready for everything from silence to incredulity to anger. My bad.

The experience was like hearing popcorn popping. "My family." "I'm healthy." "My friends." "My religion." "The woman who comes on Sunday and leads our workout." "Coffee." And more. Finally, "I would be dead from drugs by now if I weren't in prison." I must have slumped back into my chair so much that one inmate asked, "Are you OK?"

## Something To Believe in in Prison
(POSTED 30 DECEMBER 2016)

In PRP, we teach that our ego patterns—designed to keep us safe, but without any regard to making us happy—imprison, enslave, or cage us in repeated, unconsciously-driven reactivity. Most of that is scapegoating others, situations, and anything but ourselves for our problems. The basic problem is not taking responsibility for our negative feelings because we have not been taught how to recognize and deal with them.

Becoming aware of our egos' scapegoating enables us to self-regulate. Thus, the wording Response-Ability in the title Prison Response-Ability Project. We gain the ability to respond to what situations/life call for, not just react in egoic self-protection.

In this week's session, we had a few earlier group graduates attend to talk about their self-experiences in dealing with their repeated personality patterns. I was delighted to hear an inmate named Phil say to the other inmates, "I now realize that I am what stands between me and my own happiness."

## Forgiveness in Prison
### (POSTED 12 FEBRUARY 2017)

We are in our third eight-week session, with ten inmates new to the Catholic Studies Program. I still see many of the inmates from my first two sessions because they remain in Catholic Studies. (Incidentally, an inmate is not required to be Catholic nor intend to be Catholic to be in Catholic Studies.)

An inmate named Terry from an earlier session was the target of a gang-initiated attack. I understand that the attacker was required to carry out the attack by his gang leadership…or else. Terry was cold-cocked in the jaw, knocked unconscious, his head hit the floor, and he was admitted to OSU hospital in Columbus.

Weeks later, the attacker joined Catholic Studies. And, ended up in class with Terry, his victim! Expecting some trouble, the Director of Catholic Studies spoke to the now recovered victim. Terry said, "No problem. I know he was forced to do it. So, I am not angry with him."

## A Lifetime Plan in Prison
### (POSTED 6 NOVEMBER 2017)

Driving to Lebanon Correctional last week for the final night of the most recent session, I was both hopeful and anxious. The journaling assignment for the inmates was to state what they had learned about themselves and what were their plans. I was hopeful to hear about the learnings and plans generally, but anxious about one inmate.

Well into the second year of ending these eight-week sessions using this journaling assignment, I have been generally gratified to hear what the inmates say. This time, though, I had an inmate named Gary with a lifetime sentence. Propriety prohibiting too much detail, when Gary went to prison the CD player had not been invented and, now, he qualifies for a senior discount.

What could Gary's plan possibly be?

He talked about how he had learned that he puts up walls between himself and others. He said, recently, being more open, "things have gotten easier for me." Weighing into my fear, I asked him what his plan was.

Gary got a big grin and announced that he just had a hearing and was deemed eligible for parole in one year.

## Prisoners Helping Prisoners
### (POSTED 19 JULY 2018)

Into my third year presenting my project at Lebanon Correctional, my current group of 14 inmates includes 5 past students. We're two sessions in and they are taking over, in a very positive way.

Not only are they helping first-timers understand the material, in the process, I learn better ways to explain myself. Moreover, they enforce the "respect the man" rule, discouraging cross conversations when one person has the floor.

## Taking Care of Yourself in Prison
### (POSTED 2 JANUARY 2019)

This week, an inmate named Otis, in talking about his personality type, gained an insight about why he gets in trouble and gets disciplined every so often. Otis's type is often called the Helper because of the desire to become indispensable to others in order to earn their love—even though love, being by definition unconditional, cannot be earned. Attachment can be earned, but not love.

His fellow inmates acknowledged that he is always there for them. But, in order to help others so readily, the Helper must repress his or her feelings, needs, wants, desires, etc. Repressing one's own feelings works only so long. Eventually, feelings demand to be dealt with and arise as acting out, illness, or the like.

Otis now realizes that while he can "help and repress" for several months, those dark periods in which he gets in trouble are inevitable. Inevitable, unless he learns to take care of himself too. The fundamental principle comes from the second great commandment, "Thou shalt love thy neighbor as thyself," as interpreted by Fr. Richard Rohr to, "You shall love your neighbor as YOU LOVE yourself." Like Mose Allison (and Van Morrison covering Mose) sings in his song Benediction, "Thank God for self-love."

## Honoring Rituals in Prison
### (POSTED 18 APRIL 2019)

You know those certificates we occasionally receive acknowledging attendance at or completion of a seminar or mini-course? In my prison work, I have tried to honor my own advice that good leaders are greedy for feedback. So, I have more and more at the end of sessions asked the inmates questions about what works for them and what doesn't. One comment garnered quick support among the inmates; they really appreciate those certificates of completion we mostly throw in a drawer and forget.

So this past session, I promised certificates for completion of their workbooks, a mere two pages of fill-in-the-blanks and journaling before each of nine sessions, and good attendance. On a beginning roster of 15, we had about a dozen regular attendees.

For the eight who had good attendance and completed their workbooks, I created certificates on parchment, put my gold embossed Notary Public stamp on them, put them in linen folders with gold stamped designs, had the Director sign and present them.

To my surprise, most of the inmates proudly partook in the ritual and rose out of their chairs when the Director approached to hand out certificates.

## What if Prisoners were Human Beings with Hope?
### (POSTED 25 AUGUST 2016)

We finished the first Prison Responsibility Project session at Lebanon Correctional—"Club Leb" as one inmate likes to call the institution. Every participant wrote a thank you note. Let me share two excerpts.

*"Thank you for taking time to come in and help us prisoners understand who we are individually and personality-wise. One would never consider prisoners being taught to identify certain mental triggers that cause toxic emotions to surface; not to mention, the prospect of learning to deal with those emotions and letting them go. The books aren't just for us to read, but to study throughout our lives, especially if we find ourselves back in the self-made hell we worked so hard to climb out of.*

*"Thank you once again for sharing a part of you with us; and for treating us not as prisoners, but as human beings."*

*"Thanks so much for helping me learn more about myself and understanding who I am. I'm so grateful to God for bringing you into my life. You brought to me a new feeling of hope."*

# CHAPTER 8

# Culture: The Wolverine
# and the Antelope in Prison

*In individuals, insanity is rare; but in groups,
parties, nations and epochs, it is the rule.*

NIETZCHE

This chapter includes realities of prison I would want someone to warn
me about if I ever were incarcerated. There are hard facts of prison life
that inmates have to learn to cope with quickly.

### The Wolverine and the Antelope in Prison
(POSTED 6 JANUARY 2018)

At Lebanon Correctional, cellmates are assigned and roughly half the
time, seem to just tolerate each other. The other half of the time, they
look out for each other. In my current group, I had a pair of the later.
One is tall, lean and passive, like an antelope. The other is short, sturdy
and with a demeanor that says, "Don't trifle with me," like a wolverine.

They became cellies when the Wolverine heard the Antelope yelling
for help from his cell. Most inmates would avoid getting involved, but
the Wolverine has an inherent sense of justice and came to his aide. He
found the Antelope's then cellmate naked and trying to molest him.
They got the Commanding Officer for the cell block to let them change
assignments and become cellmates.

Both always came to class having carefully completed their journaling
and reading assignments. They sat next to each other and helped each
other understand the material. However, when the Antelope was assigned
to a prison facility closer to his home the Wolverine no longer completed
even a single assignment.

The Wolverine explained that like a pair of brothers they would divvy
up tasks based on preference and skills and that but for the Antelope he

would not have done any homework.

POSTSCRIPT: This was conclusively proven when I rotated around to the Wolverine's group recently. While pleasant and cooperative, he does not do homework.

## Being Strong Enough to Look Weak in Prison
### (POSTED 10 JULY 2016)

Lebanon Correctional is where inmates with a history of discipline problems often end up. Getting in trouble with another inmate is quite easy. In the Prison Response-Ability Project we talk about having the awareness to redirect our attention from, often, anger triggered by someone else to a healthy goal.

Last week, one of my inmates told me of walking away from trouble—which can look like weakness in prison—by turning his attention to his goal of getting out so he could be with his daughter.

## Name Calling in Prison
### (POSTED 7 OCTOBER 2016)

Inmates value not only the instruction they get during their two hours with us every Wednesday evening, they value the respect they receive.

Before we got started this week, one of them talked about how they are addressed in prison, that is, by what name they are called. They have name tags. I call them by their first names as written, or nickname, if known. So, more than one with a name like Ronald, whose friends call him Ronnie, has said to me he likes the way I call him Ronald. It makes him feel respected.

The guards and other inmates usually call them by their last names. I learned, though, that an easy way for a guard or staff—staff, such as the outside management firm that runs the cafeteria employing inmates—to show disrespect is to call one of them "inmate."

The inmates have ways of getting back, though, with a little repartee. One said he responds to "inmate," saying, "I prefer to be called 'prisoner' because that makes it totally clear that I am being held against my will." Getting the last word is a good antidote to disrespect.

## Ironing in Prison
### (POSTED 7 JANUARY 2017)

Our inmates live on one of about eight cellblocks, each controlled by a commanding officer. They have to be released from their individual cellblocks to come to our programs. To be out of a cellblock and traveling through the main hallway inmates must wear their dark blue slacks and light blue shirts.

There are understandably few opportunities for self-expression through clothing in prison. One, however, is ironing. Every cellblock provides an iron and ironing board.

My PRP inmates run the gamut in ironing—or not—their shirts. So, at one extreme many prefer the Bohemian style, which is not ironing at all, right out of the laundry bag. There is also the Traditionalist, basic ironing with no creases. I've noticed also the Weight Trainer look, a well-ironed shirt one size too small. Trending to the fussy extreme is the Perfectionist with razor sharp creases, the Soldier with a vertical crease on each front panel, and Individualist who irons diagonal creases or other designs into the body of the shirt.

## Recreational Outrage in Prison
### (POSTED 25 AUGUST 2017)

I notice that many inmates easily find issues about which to be outraged. You might say recreationally outraged.

Last night, as we were getting started, I was asking about the different jobs my inmates hold. One said he prints the annual corner license plate stickers for vanity and sponsored license plates. Another blurted, "Can you believe you get charged $45 dollars for that sticker and he gets paid only 34 cents an hour." (Of course, I pointed out that the sticker is only proof of a tax payment.)

That comment reminded me when another inmate got ahold of the quality report for Lebanon Correctional water works. He was outraged at the chemicals and elements found in their water. (I looked and noticed that the report showed all levels to be well below EPA Maximum Contaminant Levels. I got home and looked at the 2016 quality report for my water works…same deal: trace lead, copper and barium, to name a few.)

Also, normally the director brings candy for us to distribute during our programs, but—as always in prison—there are strict rules. Those had been abused, including by one of my inmates last week. So, the director did not bring candy this week. Guess who was outraged?

I realized that outrage is a bit endemic to prison. Seems to me being stuck in prison contributes. Since recreational outrage is not limited to prisoners, what prison are we stuck in when we are easily outraged?

## When I Walk Through that Prison Door
### (POSTED 1 SEPTEMBER 2017)

Ending an 8-week session, I complimented my group on their diligence, both in class and in their preparation for class. One inmate named Keith in particular showed great progress in sharing his emotions, feelings and background. I asked him if he planned to continue progressing in that regard. Keith said yes, but…

"When I walk through that door—from the classrooms back into the prison—emotions and feelings don't work." Others confirmed that even mere courtesy may be taken as a sign of weakness. Everett, a long-time inmate and a lifer said, "Yes, but that does not mean you have to go around being rude to everyone."

## Not Playing in Prison
### (POSTED 21 SEPTEMBER 2017)

I continue to learn about the prison culture (which doesn't seem to prepare one to return to the general culture).

Homework for this week's session was to journal on the question, "How has my personality type caused me difficulty this week?" I go around the room and give each inmate a chance to share.

One described how he got angry and offered to fight someone who was "playing with me." A little uncertain what "playing" was, I asked what the other inmate did. He described garden variety verbal jousting that my inmates do with each other all the time. I learned, though, that inmates who know someone well "can play with me," but this other inmate did not know him well enough to be allowed to "play."

So, I asked, "What's the big deal? It's just words." The whole group jumped in, explaining that in prison you can't let someone do that. Passivity looks weak. Then, the sharing inmate said, "So, I told him I'm going to my cell."

I said, "Good, I think you were wise to avoid a fight." The whole group—except me—erupted in laughter! I quickly learned that when inmates decide to fight they go to one of their cells and other inmates on the block stand guard outside the designated cell to let them fight it out and, of course, hide the fight from the guards.

## Snitching in Prison
### (POSTED 12 DECEMBER 2018)

I've heard the phrase, "Snitches get stitches" even out of prison. An inmate from one of the other groups in Catholic Studies came in to make an announcement at the behest of the Director of Prison Ministries. My group reacted very negatively to him, as a person, not because of his message.

I asked them when he left about why they let him bother them so much. There were some lame comments about him thinking he was better than everyone else. I pressed more and finally one of them disclosed what was truly behind their disdain, he was considered a snitch. He has a reputation for offering damning info about others.

We were talking about making prison wine right before he came in and they advised that if he had heard me he would have reported that I was encouraging wine making. One inmate related the story of how he, himself, ended up in prison to exemplify the no-snitch ethic.

He was one of four men in a room when a fifth man was stabbed. None would serve as a witness against another. All four went to prison. Moreover, he ended up with a much longer sentence than the rest of the four because of his prior convictions. No complaints; he carries his silence like a badge of honor.

## Two Choices in Prison
(POSTED 24 MAY 2018)

This week, we talked about some of the ego triggering events encountered in prison. A simple example is waiting in line to use the phone in any given cell block. Commonly, other inmates will try to find ways to jump line.

A couple of inmates explained that in those situations, they've got only two choices: completely passive or completely aggressive. Passive means saying and doing nothing. Aggressive means ready to fight and end up in solitary for a few days.

## Cabin Fever in Prison
(POSTED 12 APRIL 2018)

This week, I started a new session. Beyond the normal energy in starting a new group, the inmates seemed in good spirits. February was the last time I had been in this particular facility, and at the time there were extra restrictions and tensions due to gang violence.

I commented on their mood and found out that the weather had finally gotten to the point where—just that afternoon—the inmates had been able to go outside to the prison yard. (Inmates do not have winter coats. So, waiting for the temperature to rise is necessary.) They could not remember the exact date they had last been outside, but probably October.

## Boredom vs Fear in Prison
(POSTED 23 FEBRUARY 2018)

Inmates in Lebanon Correctional, a Level 3 & 4 prison, constantly experience fear. They would say the only place they could let their guard down was in the Education Room during our programs. One of my inmates came in with injuries from a sucker punch, one did not come at all because being near a fight put him in the hole (later exonerated), and another did not come because he checked into the hole for self-protection. That was life in a Level 3 & 4 institution.

The nearby unit I am presenting in now is Level 1. My rough understanding of Level 1 is there are three requirements: 1. Non-violent first offender, 2. Less than 6-year sentence, and 3. Over 35 years in age. There is some exercise equipment, there is access to an outdoor area, and there is a GED program. The building has two large, open dormitory rooms with a common area in between. Inmates move around freely, seemingly like a high school at lunch time.

On the other hand, there is very little programming such as ours sponsored by the Archdiocese Prison Ministry. Also, jobs do not seem as available. Thus, while fear is not a common experience for them, boredom is.

To those of us with busy work days—one following another, exercise equipment, outdoor activities, reading, and playing cards might sound like fun...occasionally. Inmates liken their experience to the movie Ground Hog Day. The same day, the same place, over and over.

## Believing in Yourself Despite Being in Prison
(POSTED 13 FEBRUARY 2019)

I started a new session recently debuting a 2nd level course with a group of thirteen: eight 1st level graduates and five inmates new to Catholic Studies. The 2nd level course builds on the 1st level course. So, the five inexperienced inmates were understandably playing catch-up.

Experienced inmates volunteered to tutor the inexperienced and began helping even during the first class. Nonetheless, as I walked everyone through the workbook and the requirements, some new inmates began grumbling about how much work was assigned and how complex the information was.

I stood up in the middle of the circle of seated inmates and gave my best Knute Rockne speech. I told them I gave them so much work and made the material so advanced because I believe in them. And, they should believe more in themselves.

My words landed well on the majority. In the end, I handed out ten certificates of completion. But I could never figure out how to reach everyone. I even had to recommend that two inmates be dismissed from our programming completely.

# CHAPTER 9

# Songs and Poems:
# I Created My Own Prison

*Poetry is news from the frontiers of consciousness.*
LAWRENCE FERLINGHETTI

Not surprisingly, I have found poetry, including the lyrics to popular music, helpful even though Lebanon Correctional does not permit me to bring in any electronic equipment to actually play music. Surprisingly, there are a wealth of lyrics reminding us that our troubles are likely to be of our own making, specifically; prisons, chains, slavery, cages, cells, etc. of our own making. Hearing this message repeated in popular culture is meaningful to the inmates.

## Prison of Our Own Making
### (POSTED 27 OCTOBER 2017)

In the Prison Response-Ability Project, the recurring theme is how we put ourselves in prisons of our own making. The concept is that simple and that hard.

Simple because we have the key, namely, awareness. Hard because our minds are so trapped and distracted by busyness we don't have the ability to utilize the key, namely, presence.

Our situation might be described as we don't even have the presence to begin to be present. And look at all of the poets, prophets, artists and guides who keep trying to remind us. Some of my favorites:

Bruce Springsteen, "Living Proof," *Lucky Town* album.

*You shot through my anger, you shot through my rage*
*To show me my prison was just an open cage*
*There were no keys no guards*
*Oh, just one frightened man and some old shadows for bars*

Bill Wilson, Alcoholics Anonymous, Third Step Prayer

*God, I offer myself to Thee—to build with me and to do with me as Thou wilt. Relieve me of the bondage of self, that I may better do Thy will. Take away my difficulties, that victory over them may bear witness to those I would help of Thy Power, Thy Love, and Thy Way of life. May I do Thy will always. Amen*

Richard Lovelace, "To Althea From Prison"

*Stone walls do not a prison make,*
*Nor iron bars a cage;*
*Minds innocent and quiet take*
*That for an hermitage;*
*If I have freedom in my love*
*And in my soul am free,*
*Angels alone, that soar above,*
*Enjoy such liberty*

Young The Giant, "Something To Believe In"

*I'll give you something to believe in*
*Burn up the basement full of demons*
*Realize you're a slave to your mind, break free*

Bob Marley, "Redemption Song"

*Emancipate yourself from mental slavery*
*None but our self can free our mind*

## Rock Rap in Prison
### (POSTED 27 OCTOBER 2017)

The inmates in my project get a workbook to use. The Workbook is organized into eight sections just like the course. The sections start with the lyrics to popular works of music chosen because they include lines about how we lock ourselves in prisons or cages of our own making.

Last week's song was "Already Gone" by the Eagles. The key lyrics are,

*Well I know it wasn't you who held me down*
*Heaven knows it wasn't you who set me free*

*So often times it happens that we live our lives in chains*
*And we never even know we have the key*

We start the session with my having someone read the lyrics. The inmates tend to be younger and more familiar with Rap music. So, this 1974 Rock song was not familiar to most of them. The inmate who volunteered to read/sing the lyrics naturally used the versing he liked…Rap.

I just wish I could have recorded this Rap Rock version. Some sections actually sounded appropriate for Rap. Imagine Notorious B.I.G. intoning:

*And I'm already gone*
*And I'm feelin' strong*
*I will sing this vict'ry song, woo, hoo,*
*hoo, woo, hoo, hoo*

## The Elephant in the Room in Prison
### (POSTED 20 DECEMBER 2019)

We reviewed Rumi's poem, "The Guest House." Rumi focuses on the dark thought (fear), the shame, and the malice (anger) that come to visit us. They are the guests he is writing about.

Rumi exhorts us to treat them as welcomed guests. They are actually sources of intelligence and will tell us something important if we listen to them. But, as mere guests, after we have welcomed them and listened to them, we must expect them to go on their way.

### "The Guest House" by Jellaludin Rumi

*This being human is a guest house.*
*Every morning a new arrival.*
*A joy, a depression, a meanness,*
*some momentary awareness comes*
*as an unexpected visitor*

*Welcome and entertain them all!*
*Even if they are a crowd of sorrows,*
*who violently sweep your house*
*empty of its furniture,*

*still, treat each guest honorably.*
*He may be clearing you out*
*for some new delight.*

*The dark thought, the shame, the malice,*
*meet them at the door laughing and invite them in.*
*Be grateful for whatever comes.*
*because each has been sent*
*as a guide from beyond.*

While all of us experience all three: fear, shame, and anger; we typically prioritize one over the other two. After reading the poem, a fear-type personality inmate understandably described his dark thought as the "elephant in EVERY room." Figuring out who can be trusted in what situation is a 24/7 task in prison. Fear in prison is "the guest who stayed too long."

## "Multiple Numbers" in Prison
### (POSTED 7 SEPTEMBER 2018)

Many of the inmates in the course have "multiple numbers." Each time a person is imprisoned anew, he is assigned a new inmate number. So, about someone imprisoned for a fifth time, a fellow inmate might say, "He has five numbers."

This week was our last class; a new session with a new group starts next week. We covered what each inmate learned, how he would use that knowledge, and what was his plan. The reading this week related well to our topic.

### Autobiography In Five Short Chapters

*Chapter I* — *I walk down the street. There is a deep hole in the sidewalk. I fall in. I am lost... I am hopeless. It isn't my fault. It takes forever to find a way out.*

*Chapter II* — *I walk down the same street. There is a deep hole in the sidewalk. I pretend I don't see it. I fall in again. I can't believe I am in this same place. But it isn't my fault. It still takes a long time to get out.*

*Chapter III* — *I walk down the same street. There is a deep hole in the sidewalk. I see it there. I still fall in... it's a habit... but, my eyes are open. I know where I am. It is my fault. I get out immediately.*

*Chapter IV* — *I walk down the same street. There is a deep hole in the sidewalk. I walk around it.*

*Chapter V* — *I walk down another street.*

Portia Nelson, *There's a Hole in My Sidewalk: The Romance of Self-Discovery*

## Letting People Out of Prison
### (POSTED 18 NOVEMBER 2016)

There are plenty of popular songs acknowledging prisons of our own making. We use one each session.

"Living Proof" by Bruce Springsteen

> *You shot through my anger*
> *You shot through my rage*
> *To show me my prison was just an open cage*
> *There were no keys no guards*
> *Just one frightened man and some old shadows for bars*

"Wish You Were Here" by Pink Floyd

> *Did you exchange a walk-on part in the war for a lead role in a cage?*

"Hotel California" by The Eagles

> *And she said, "We are all just prisoners here, of our own device."*

"My Own Prison" by Creed

> *I cry out to God seeking only his decision.*
> *Gabriel stands and confirms*
> *I've created my own prison.*

"The Prisoner" by The Clash

> *I look to my left.*
> *I look to my right.*
> *And, I'm looking for a man.*

*I'm looking for a sign.*
*I don't wanna be the prisoner.*
*I don't wanna be the prisoner.*
*I don't wanna be the prisoner*

"Mama Tried" by Merle Haggard

*And I turned twenty-one in prison doing life without parole.*
*No one could steer me right but Mama tried,*
*Mama tried. Mama tried to raise me better, but her pleading I denied*
*That leaves only me to blame 'cause Mama tried*

"Longview" by Greenday

*I locked the door to my own cell*
*And I lost the key*

"Already Gone" by The Eagles

*Well I know it wasn't you who held me down*
*Heaven knows it wasn't you who set me free*
*So often times it happens that we live our lives in chains*
*And we never even know we have the key*

"One" by Metallica

*Darkness imprisoning me*
*All that I see*
*Absolute horror*
*I cannot live*
*I cannot die*
*Trapped in myself*
*Body my holding cell*

"Stuck In A Moment You Can't Get Out Of" by U2

*You've got to get yourself together*
*You've got stuck in a moment*
*And now you can't get out of it*

*Don't say that later will be better*
*Now you're stuck in a moment*
*And you can't get out of it*

"Rusty Cage" by Soundgarden, covered by Johnny Cash

*I'm gonna break, I'm gonna break my, Gonna break my rusty cage and run.*

"Redemption Song" by Bob Marley

*Emancipate yourselves from mental slavery;*
*None but ourselves can free our mind.*

"Something To Believe In" by Young The Giant

*I'll give you something to believe in*
*Burn up a basement full of demons*
*Realize you're a slave to your mind, break free*
*Now give me something to believe in*
*Promise me*
*See, I'm afraid*
*I'm a slave to my mind*
*You give me something to believe in*

# CHAPTER 10

# The Enneagram: Discussing Homer's *The Iliad* and *The Odyssey* in Prison

*The testimony of the greatest humans who have ever lived is that the way to make the most of ourselves is by transcending ourselves.*

DON RICHARD RISO

The Enneagram personality model is the core of my work in and out of prison. So, the joke that tells itself is that I use the same materials in my work with executives and felons!

For those not familiar with the Enneagram, simply stated, in Greek, ennea means nine and gram can be translated to list. Thusly, a list of nine personality types. Each type is described in two ways below, one prosaic and one poetic.

## Discussing Homer's *The Iliad* and *The Odyssey* in Prison
### (POSTED 15 MAY 2017)

In the program, we use the Enneagram personality model to help inmates move from reactivity to "response-ability." (See, www.theenneagramin-business.com) Using the Enneagram, inmates gain self-awareness of their habits of personality.

The Enneagram pattern shows up over and over in various times and cultures. We discuss the historical origins in the first sessions of the PRP. Among places the nine Enneagram types show up is in Homer's *The Odyssey*.

Mentioning *The Iliad* and *The Odyssey* in any group—in or out of prison—I don't assume familiarity with the works or even the names. The education and, I'm sure, the intelligence of my inmates varies widely. I've seen graduate degrees, a Japanese speaker, a former president of a union, for example. I've had inmates struggling with the math necessary to obtain their GEDs.

When I referred to *The Odyssey* with my current group, I was happy to hear one inmate speak up right away and show his familiarity. He was even familiar with the nine peoples Odysseus and his crew visited on the return to Ithaca from the Trojan Wars. Moreover, for the benefit of the class, he was able to describe each of the nine peoples and I, then, related each to their Enneagram type.

## Recognizing Our Own Prisons
### (POSTED 18 NOVEMBER 2016)

The key theme of the Prison Response-Ability Project is learning that what stands between us and almost anything we want is primarily ourselves. The Enneagram has roots in, among other places, fourth century Christianity and a monk named Evagrius. His monastic community individually contemplated what stood between themselves and the divine. The barriers were always themselves, but in a variety of ways which Evagrius identified and which became known as the seven deadly sins. These along with the vices of vanity and fear informed the development of the nine Enneagram personality types.

The seven deadly sins plus two—vanity and fear—turn out to be readily familiar to most inmates. Each Enneagram personality type is identified closely with one of those nine. I find the inmates have little trouble identifying which is his most present deadly sin. Recognizing one's deadly sin is the pathway to understanding one's Enneagram type and one's prison of his own making.

## The Prison of Always Needing to be Right
### (POSTED 10 NOVEMBER 2017)

This Wednesday, we started my "201 level" course based on the book, THE ENNEAGRAM A CHRISTIAN PERSPECTIVE by Richard Rohr OFM, formerly of Cincinnati and Roger Bacon High School, the high school I attended. This course has nine sessions, one for each of the nine Enneagram ego structures, commonly called types or personalities. These sessions have me discussing the week's type with the person(s) of that type and other inmates occasionally asking questions.

Completion of the "101 level" course is a prerequisite and this enables me to fill the class with at least one of each of the nine types. We start with Type One, The Perfectionist, and work our way through the types in numerical order.

This week's Perfectionist was a near classic example. They are in search of perfection resulting in them constantly judging others—and themselves—against idealistic and, perhaps, unrealistic standards. This perfectionist inmate can't help but notice what's wrong. "Wrong," including something that is only 99% right.

For example, I convert the room from classroom style to meeting style before the inmates arrive, simply moving tables and chairs around. Eric, my perfectionist will always make adjustments when he arrives, straightening or, this week, deciding we needed four tables instead of the normal three. Later, I said something lightly to the group along the lines, "You boys need to understand…." Eric corrected me, saying, "You mean you Men…" He has said before that what got him into trouble is that he would not listen to what others were trying to tell him.

We all know someone fussy like Eric who always has to be right.

*There once was a One so right*
*About the trivial he would fight*
*Others he would judge*
*His opinions would not budge*
*When he neared all would take flight*

## The Prison of Always Needing to be Indispensable
### (POSTED 16 NOVEMBER 2017)

This week we featured Type Two, The Giver.

James the Giver proudly helps others expecting help in return. Like all nine Enneagram types, the approach just doesn't work all the time. Being a Giver in prison seems especially difficult. For example, James related a number of examples of him giving something of his to help someone but not getting the slightest reciprocation and yet feeling obliged to continue giving.

With a strategy that does not work, especially in prison, the Giver is left with only his pride. Givers in and out of prison are prone to proudly noticing and talking about others not behaving as nicely as them. James—who is in prison for breaking and entering and assault of his drug dealer—warned me to be careful of another inmate because he was in prison for robbery.

His pride showing, he pointed out that he would never do such a thing as robbery, seeing such as clearly worse than breaking and entering and assault.

We all know someone like James who always has to be proudly helping others and will not ask for help in return.

*There once was a helper Type Two*
*Who thought of only you, you and you*
*Behind his help was pride*
*Self-care he would not abide*
*He wondered when his day off was due*

## The Prison of Always Needing to be Doing
### (POSTED 24 NOVEMBER 2017)

This week we featured Type Three, The Performer.

The Performer constantly seeks validation for doing, for winning, for looking successful. Performers worship at the To Do list alter. Like all nine Enneagram types, the approach just doesn't work all the time. Constantly doing for doing's sake leaves them as what we call "human doings" rather than human beings; they lose touch with their feelings.

In two plus years in prisons, I never had a Three inmate. So, I had to recruit Steve, another volunteer. He was delighted to hear that I have not come across an inmate Three. Of course, he was thinking that was because Three's don't end up in prison. I did not choose to point out to him that Threes may well be in prison but their vanity prevents them from entering self-development programs. Why would such a successful person need self-improvement?

We all know someone like Steve who is blessed with an over-abundance of energy and always has to be doing something.

*There once was a Three indeed productive*
*With charms oh so seductive*

*He lived for success*
*He liked failure quite less*
*For him approval was superconductive*

## The Prison of Always Needing to be Special
### (POSTED 30 NOVEMBER 2017)

This week we featured Type Four, The Individualist.

The Individualist constantly seeks a special identity to salve a gnawing sense that he or she is missing something others have. This longing often inspires poetry and song. Clapton, Hendrix and Dylan are considered Type Fours. However, someone new always shows up with something the Four envies.

One of my fours named Glenn constantly reminds me and the rest of the class that he does not care what we and other people think of him. Last night was the right time for me to ask Glenn, "If you don't care what I think of you why do you keep telling me that I should think of you as someone who doesn't care?" His stunned and sad reaction made me feel I may have gone too far. True to Type, Glenn readily experiences deep rejection.

We all know someone like Glenn who always has to look, act, and be thought of as special.

*There once was a special Type Four*
*Who found everyone else to be a bore*
*    He feared rejection*
*    So for protection*
*To those who got close he showed the door*

## The Prison of Merely Observing
### (POSTED 7 DECEMBER 2017)

This week we featured Type Five, The Observer.

The Observer worries that life itself will drain the life out of them. So, they are careful to conserve their energy and emotions. Usually, they tend to be good at conserving information also, having great memories.

Eventually, Fives can withdraw so much that they become isolated from others and from their own feelings. I often find humor in asking

Fives how they FEEL about something. The answer will usually begin, "I THINK…" Fives often find others' questions intrusive.

Sam, my featured Five this week, reflected sadly on how he responded when his mother would ask questions such as, "What happened at school today?" Sam said he wished now that he would have responded more openly rather than his standard, "Nuthin'."

We all know someone like Sam who always takes it all in, while way less comes out.

*There once was a quiet man Type Five*
*So emotionless he seemed barely alive*
  *His energy he saved*
  *Claims of aloofness he braved*
*While his mind did buzz like a hive*

## The Prison of Always Needing More Certainty
### (POSTED 9 APRIL 2019)

Last week at Lebanon Correctional in the Prison Response-Ability Project course, we featured Type Six. The Loyal/Skeptic constantly, but skeptically, seeks grounding and certainty, often finding solace in rules, procedures and more learning. Worry about what life is going to bring keeps the Six's mind mostly in the future.

This carefulness works well only some of the time. Sixes can struggle with decision-making, even when they have clarity regarding the issues, facts and options, because they seek unattainable certainty.

Ironically, if the Sixes got the certainty they seek, life would be so predictable as to resemble the movie *Ground Hog Day*.

We all know someone like me (Yes, like me.) who always worries about what is going to happen.

*There once was a Six not feeling supported*
*Any decision he made would be aborted*
  *Others he did not trust*
  *Grounding he did lust*
*His projections of others were distorted*

## The Prison of Always Needing More Fun
### (POSTED 6 JANUARY 2018)

This week we featured Type Seven. The Enthusiast constantly seeks fun and interesting experiences. Avoidance of painful tedium keeps the Enthusiast mind looking to the future planning for positive possibilities.

Eventually, hastiness and intemperance result in difficulties. They can have great trouble getting tasks and projects completed because of their blinkered desire to start new endeavors instead.

Chris, my Seven inmate, has put his need for newness to good use. While a journeyman bricklayer, in prison, he is getting training in cooking. He'll read any book I give him and he rivals my addiction to crossword puzzles. Chris has had 100% attendance when in my courses.

We all know someone like Chris who always wants more fun and more options.

*There once was a Seven full of innovations*
*Life was fun, frolic and creations*
*    Not taking time to think*
*    Into trouble he would sink*
*"It could have been worse" were his rationalizations.*

## The Prison of Always Needing Control
### (POSTED 11 JANUARY 2018)

This week we featured Enneagram Type Eight. The Challenger constantly seeks to have a big impact which feels to others like controlling and, sometimes, bullying. They tend to speak in challenging syntax, such as, "Why would you do that?" I have a soon-to-be four granddaughter who shows signs of being a Challenger even at her early age. Recently, when I was visiting, after having declined when asked if she wanted something to eat, she shortly thereafter came into the kitchen and said to four adults in a demanding tone, "Is anybody going to fix me any dinner?"

Eventually, people tend to want the Challenger to have a comeuppance. The Challenger senses this resistance and becomes even stronger—often louder. An Eight can have a self-righteous sense of justice which turns into revenge.

John, my Challenger inmate, has one more year on a thirty-year sentence. When we talked about forgiveness and letting go of revenge, he visibly tightened up and said, "I think about getting revenge *every* day." His normal demeanor clearly says, "Do not trifle with me!"

We all know someone like John who always wants to be in control.

*There once was an Eight so bold*
*Who feared of being controlled*
   *Others he would protect*
   *Some wanted to ring his neck*
*Be vulnerable he could not be told*

## The Prison of Controlling by Not Doing
### (POSTED 28 DECEMBER 2017)

This week we featured Type Six...Whoops, sorry, Type Nine. I had two Sixes in the group, but one got assigned to a different prison and the other must have been in a cell block that got locked down due to the high amount of gang violence lately. I knew my Type Nine would be the most able to step in. In fact, he had long ago completed the work for all nine sessions.

The Mediator is constantly seeking harmony in all things. Avoidance of conflict and avoidance in general is the Mediator's primary technique. But eventually, avoidance becomes acquiescence, acquiescence becomes unresponsive, and unresponsive becomes self-negating. The Nine disappears while, paradoxically, getting angry and angrier about being ignored. Eventually, the anger explodes.

My Nine inmate is calming to even be around, but some time ago a guard tampered with a picture his grandmother had written on and he exploded, beating the guard's head with a padlock. The Nines are said to be like Mt. St. Helen's, blowing up very seldom and very violently.

We all know someone who always knows what to do but can't (or won't).

*There once were Nines so serene*
*Away from all conflict they would lean*

*To get them to move*
*Hard it would prove*
*For them all points of view could be seen*

## Enneagram Repeating Questions
### (POSTED 15 APRIL 2019)

We use the technique of repeating questions in Enneagram work outside of prison. Two people sit face-to-face with one repeating one of the questions written for each of the nine types. The type-specific questions are:

TYPE ONE: How do you criticize yourself?

TYPE TWO: How do you ignore your own needs?

TYPE THREE: How do you avoid failure?

TYPE FOUR: How do you compare yourself to others?

TYPE FIVE: How do you avoid your emotions?

TYPE SIX: How do you protect yourself?

TYPE SEVEN: How do you avoid pain?

TYPE EIGHT: How do you avoid vulnerability?

TYPE NINE: How do you discount your own thoughts?

I have used them in prison too, but it's a struggle. The repeating questions are repeated to invite the answerer to go deeper each time. Most inmates just can't let themselves be that vulnerable and the exercise tends to break into chaos. For example, some inmates will simply resort to answering every time, "I don't." Also, their stubbornness tends to evoke understandable laughter.

Type Fours though tend to have a more present sense of their feelings. One took the questioning very seriously. He later asked me, "Is your own type's question designed to be especially painful for you."

I had only the trite but true answer that in personal development, "No pain, no gain."

## CHAPTER 11

# Life Lessons: Words to Live by from Prison

*Though nobody can go back and make a new beginning…*
*Anyone can start over and make a new ending.*

CHICO XAVIER

I started my work in prison with the thought of giving back. I have enjoyed a life of relative abundance largely due to the help freely given to me by others. As I told the first group I worked with at the end of our nine weeks together, "You guys tricked me. I came in here to give, but I have received more than I could possibly have given."

This chapter includes life lessons which I may have already known but which were embossed in my memory by relearning them in prison.

### Words to Live by from Prison
**(POSTED 30 JANUARY 2019)**

Last week, we were going around the room talking about the journaling assignment of dealing with people of different backgrounds and worldviews.

One inmate was resisting making any comment, but I continued to press him. Finally, he blurts out as if reciting poetry...

*You know my name,*
*Not my story.*
*You've heard*
*What I've done,*
*Not what I've been through.*

## Harvard, Prison, Immigrants
(POSTED 9 MARCH 2017)

Wednesday evenings from 5:00 PM to 7:00 PM is when my sessions are held. Yesterday, before going to Lebanon, from 8:00 AM until 4:00 PM, I was at a Harvard Business School/Young President's Organization session.

The HBS/YPO attendance was well over 300 people from about sixty Cincinnati/Dayton companies. The Harvard professor, one person, commanded the room all day. He was erudite, he was funny, he was challenging, he was down-to-earth. To get 300 plus business people to stay put and off their phones all day is hard; he did it.

**Interesting fact:** He is a Russian immigrant, Boris Groysberg.

At 4:00 PM I left for Lebanon Correctional. Last night our whole Catholic Studies group of about sixty met in the prison chapel for a musical performance by a singer/song writer/musician. She was talented, strong, gentle, captivating. To get sixty prisoners to stay put and quiet for two hours is hard; she did it.

**Interesting fact:** She is a Croatian immigrant, Tajci Cameron

Come to think of it, last Friday night Sharon and I had a wonderful couples dinner night out with friends. He is a business owner. She's a lawyer.

**Interesting fact:** He is a German immigrant, She is a Mexican immigrant.

I just remembered, Monday I stopped by the integrative medical center where my daughter works. The center is one of the top ten integrative medical centers in the country and is run by a couple, both physicians.

**Interesting fact:** They are South African immigrants.

But, wait, there's more. My namesakes are two immigrants, great-great grandfather Thomas Hattersley a knife maker from Sheffield, England and great grandfather Tommy O'Connor a railroad worker from County Kerry, Ireland.

We tend to think of foreigners as other, think of different demographics as other, and inmates as other. I have found more similarity than difference in foreign travels, in those with different backgrounds, and in my prison work.

## Being Listened to in Prison
### (POSTED 14 APRIL 2017)

Last Wednesday night was a non-program week. We just finished an eight-week presentation and will start a new group next week. Instead of our session, the Director set up the chapel for confessions.

We have over sixty inmates in the Archdiocese program, plus 7 or 8 presenters. Three priests came in to hear confessions. So, rough math, two dozen confessions, non-stop for each priest.

Some inmates in the Archdiocese program are Catholic, but most not. This took extra time because the priests dealt with them one-by-one, explaining confession.

The confessions were in the open, though at a distance from the seating area. I could see the priests leaning in to listen attentively.

The priests walked out with us at the end of the night, clearly exhausted. One said, "Listening is really much harder than we think." Hmm, good point. Maybe that is why we sometimes struggle to understand each other.

## The Prison of "If Only He Would I Would"
### (POSTED 3 JULY 2017)

By day, I do business consulting, primarily executive coaching. With executives, I over use the joke: The same materials work with inmates and executives.

The reality underlying that joke is that developing "response-ability" benefits all of us. We all put ourselves in reactive prisons of our own making. We call them personalities, egos, just the way I was born. And, importantly, they protect us and enable us to progress, but only so far. In business the phrase is, What Got You Here Won't Get You There.

One religious thinker even suggests that Original Sin in Christianity may refer to the sin of ego. Sin can be transliterated to separation, and, therefore, it could be said our focus on our egos separates us from focusing on the divine.

When listening to my inmates and executives (and myself) I keep my ear attuned to signs of being locked in one's own prison. Whenever I hear words that fit the syntax, "If only he would, I would," the time is right to stop and parse out the logic. Invariably, it's faulty.

Once we say, he has to change, not me. Or, he's to blame, not me. We've walked into our personality prison cell and closed the door. The antidote to a stuck relationship is simple, the more mature person has to go first. Yes, be willing to change, be willing to take our share of the blame.

## Two Thousand Year-old Advice for Prison (and Us)
### (POSTED 4 AUGUST 2017)

My work in prison occurs primarily through conversations. Knowing that 95% of those currently in prison will get out, I am always thinking of helping the inmates become able to find and keep jobs. The prison context does not foster common courtesy. I believe that coaching them on how to courteously conduct themselves in their conversations with each other will be helpful for later in dealing with bosses, co-workers and customers.

Looking for material, I remembered Cicero's essay from 44BCE "On Duties" setting down the rules for ordinary conversation. First, he said a good conversation required "alternation" among the participants. Then, these rules:

*speak clearly;*
*speak easily but not too much, especially when others want their turn;*
*do not interrupt;*
*be courteous;*
*deal seriously with serious matters and gracefully with lighter ones;*
*never criticize people behind their backs;*
*stick to subjects of general interest;*
*do not talk about yourself;*
*and, above all, never lose your temper.*

What I've been pleased with is how the inmates respond to these concepts when presented as a set of rules. What I've not been pleased with is noticing how outside of prison these rules are roundly ignored, including by me.

## Craving a Normal Life in Prison
### (POSTED 13 SEPTEMBER 2017)

This week, my inmates journaled on the question of what they want to get out of the class. One inmate said, "I want to learn about myself which is what this course is about. But I won't lie...I come here because I crave the fellowship. Out there (in the prison), I can't be myself. I can't share my thoughts. I can't share my feelings. I can't talk about my kids. I just want to get out and...

Go to church with my family,
Go fishing with my kids,
Get a job,
Make a car payment,
Go home at the end of the day.
I have spent most of my twenties in jail.

On the way home, "Normal Life" by July For Kings came on. Some of the lyrics...

*For years I cursed these dead end streets*
*No where to go, no one to meet*
*We only talked about the crazy woman down the road*
*But everything makes much more sense now*
*Someday I'll have my own house*
*I'll make enough to make it easier to pay the phone bill*
*In the backyard playing on the swingset*
*Dark green shoes off you can get your feet wet*
*My wife and I will sit quiet in the sunroom*
*Sundown, big moon, big sky.*

## Spiritual Bypass in Prison
(POSTED 20 SEPTEMBER 2018)

Our first working session began this week with a poem by Rumi, "The Guest House." Rumi's point is that our negative emotions of fear, shame, and anger are merely our guests who need to be acknowledged and tended to and sent on their way. Each of us is a guest house, not a storage facility, for pain.

One of my inmates argued we should not even have pain, let alone acknowledge it. This approach has a name…spiritual bypass. Spiritual bypass, a phrase coined by the psychologist John Selwood, is the use of spirituality to avoid our painful feelings, unmet needs, and unhealed wounds. Spiritual bypassing happens when we are not yet ready to accept an aspect of ourselves. The un-owned aspect of self gets repressed.

We engage in spiritual bypassing when we are in denial of a fatal flaw that is glaringly obvious, or when we go deep into spiritual practices or philosophies, but, for example, we treat people poorly. Since our psychology is the problem and our spirituality is the answer, to truly heal, we must face the psychological difficulty of working with our pain, otherwise our spirituality can become merely a band-aid on a deep wound.

## Visible Invisible Barriers in Prison
(POSTED 27 JULY 2018)

I attended a talk by Peter Block last weekend. Our room was set up auditorium style when he started. He reshuffled us, making the point that how we manage space affects relationships.

For years at Lebanon Correctional, I simply used the classrooms with tables mostly as is. This week I had the tables pushed away and the chairs placed in an open circle.

The first inmate to arrive complained. The second said, "Oh, we're sitting AA style." Once we got rolling, the increased level of interaction, not just with me, was palpable.

## Back in Prison
### (POSTED 3 JUNE 2018)

I missed the last three weeks at Lebanon Correctional due to neck surgery (completely successful). Walking around in public wearing a neck brace and looking very fragile the last three weeks has been enlightening.

Strangers have gone out of their way to help me. A pregnant woman held a door for me, a man my age saw me wiggling to get out of my car and came to hold my door and even closed it for me. Seems that we are more caring when in the presence of the obviously wounded.

So, what if we recognized that we've all been wounded in some way? The first step, which is a very difficult one for inmates, is to acknowledge and talk about their wounds.

## The Prison of Past Success
### (POSTED 22 JANUARY 2018)

Our egoic personalities are designed to protect us in our own very specific ways. Our protection pattern can be very effective in the right situation and is reinforced by that success. The problem comes when we deploy our personality strategy in the wrong situation.

In my executive coaching, I see this, often dramatically, in job changes. A ready example is the star sales person promoted to sales manager who approaches management as if it were sales. The approach of constantly influencing subordinates rather than providing them with clear strategy, priorities and goals is classic. We all have heard stories of the best sales person promoted to become the worst sales manager.

I have seen this pattern with the star customer service provider promoted to customer service manager. Great customer service providers are often very accommodating with the empathy to see the other person's point of view. This accommodative, empathic approach tends to be very accepting of excuses for failure. Having succeeded at being hands-on, the new manager steps in to rescue and enable poor performers.

I've seen a star solo performer in a professional service firm who succeeded by being a very tough negotiator, always saying no and delaying, forcing his counterparts to negotiate against themselves if they want to move the deals forward. He used this same approach when promoted to run the firm to manage his direct reports, always forcing them to make the first move and not being satisfied.

We are all inmates of our pasts. Without letting go, we will make no progress. Letting go of our defensiveness is hard enough for us living normal lives, imagine how defensive incarceration makes someone. And, how long that defensiveness lasts.

## Transmitting Pain in Prison
(POSTED 25 FEBRUARY 2019)

We started a new course on self-mastery two weeks ago. The inmates tend to see themselves in their weekly journaling as having distinctly high thinking, emotional, and behavioral self-mastery. On the other hand, in our discussions, the inmates quickly see low self-mastery in others. They readily criticize guards, fellow inmates, politicians, police, etc., even with a lack of facts.

This seems to be the operation of the Leaden Rule which can be understood in contrast with the Golden Rule. The Leaden Rule, rather than adjuring, "Do unto others what we would have done unto ourselves," postulates, "Do unto others as you would least want done unto yourself." It's simple, what easier way is there to make myself feel less pain when I judge myself negatively than to notice and judge others as worse? So, inside that person gratuitously finding fault with you is a person constantly finding fault with him or herself. Indeed, take some time to notice how frequently we needlessly complain about others. Why waste the precious time and energy?

It seems, if we can't transform our pain, we transmit our pain.

## How My Granddaughter Stays Out of Prison
(POSTED 17 JULY 2017)

My inmates, perhaps not unlike the rest of us, are really affected by the labels we can put on people, even fixated at times.

One participant was gay and a few others would not sit next to him. One is Jewish—Yes, in Catholic Studies…Hooray for Vatican II—and a couple of other inmates can't help but openly refer to his faith/ethnicity even when it has not the slightest relevance.

I learned from one of my three-year old granddaughters how to avoid being labeled. She defiantly eschews being labeled. If I say you are a cutie or you are an angel, she will say, "No, I'm Harper."

How profound and innocent. Harper won't let others put her in their prison of labels.

## The Prison of Labels by Prince Ea
### (POSTED 15 JULY 2017)

*I Am NOT Black, You are NOT White.*
*These Labels were Made Up to Divide us.*

Download this Spoken Word piece here: https://itunes.apple.com/us/album/i-am-not-a-label-single/id1055051891

# CHAPTER 12

# How Inmates Think, Feel and Act: Freedom is Just Another Prison

*You never really understand a person until you consider things from his point of view—until you climb into his skin and walk around in it.*

ATTICUS FINCH

I make a living primarily predicting and improving human behavior in the workplace. I am always watching what people do and trying to understand what their unspoken thoughts and unexpressed feelings are. Prison life was brand new to me, but, ultimately, people are people.

### Freedom is Just Another Prison
#### (POSTED 14 MARCH 2019)

Last session, we were discussing other-awareness and situational-awareness. An inmate named William raised the issue of being attuned to how people from outside prison feel about being in prison and around a felon in a prison uniform. Earlier this week, William properly went to the chapel with a chapel pass in hand. There was only one other person there, a female chapel volunteer. He said, "I saw the fear in her eyes." William quickly showed her his pass and backed out of the door that he entered, waiting for the chaplain to arrive.

I complimented him on his sensitivity.

This led us to a discussion of what a former inmate's experience is once out of prison. Half or more of the group had been out. These inmates described the experience as disorienting because so much had changed, including themselves. One, Thomas, entered as an immature 18-year-old boy, barely shaving and left as a twenty-something, 260 pound, 6 foot 4, tattooed, bearded, black man.

Thomas could tell how people feared his very presence. He said, as a result, he felt that so much was off-limits to him that freedom was "just another prison."

## Lucasville and Luxury in Prison
### (POSTED 18 MAY 2018 )

The Lucasville Ohio Prison Riot was twenty-five years ago last month. By the numbers: 9 inmates dead at the hand of other inmates, 1 guard dead, 8 guards taken hostage, 10 days of rioting, 1800 inmates in a facility built for 1540, $40 million in damage, 21 prisoner demands agreed to be reviewed.

One of the inmates named Frank was there. He has been incarcerated now for 36 years. He told me earlier that the reason inmates fight over small things is that they have so little to begin with. I asked Frank to tell me more about that this week.

Among Frank's comments was the claim that the young inmates today don't appreciate what Lucasville did for them. He said they now have "luxuries" such as microwaves and ice machines, bigger cells, and individual shower stalls.

## Perspective Taking in Prison
### (POSTED 30 AUGUST 2018)

Our topic this week was trying to understand someone else's perspective, a key learning in emotional intelligence and pivotal in moving from reactivity to response-ability. The inmates commonly perceive the corrections officers as bullies.

I engaged Frank (formerly of Lucasville Prison and mentioned above)—who admittedly has anger issues and is very sensitive to being disrespected—in a discussion of taking the guards' perspective. He is truly trying to be a good citizen and, for example, is the most knowledgeable of the Bible in the current group. Try as I might, and as others in the group tried, he could not find any empathy, understanding, or acceptance of what might make a guard behave as a bully.

Frank related a time when he was pulled into the captain's office and felt disrespected and looked down upon. I asked him what about "Love thy neighbor as thyself." He said the Bible does not apply in that situation. He would not budge. He was so adamant that he was out of his chair making his case as class ended.

Taking his perspective, as we know, he was in the Lucasville Prison riots over 25 years ago.

## Leadman in Prison
### (POSTED 6 OCTOBER 2018)

Starting this week's session with my normal request for any good news, one inmate, Richard, was eager to relate that he had been promoted to leadman in the license tag distribution shop. License plates, annual stickers, handicap tags, etc. come from LCI.

Richard proudly elaborated that he is now one of only three inmates who can stuff envelopes for handicap hangtags. "What's so special?" I asked. The three thereby have access to personal addresses, something an inmate normally can't see.

Taking pride in one's trusted position in an organization is something I've seen in and out of prison, but, candidly, did not expect to see when I first entered Lebanon Correctional.

## What Prisoners Talk About
### (POSTED 30 SEPTEMBER 2018)

A friend accompanied me this week to a session. This was his first time in a prison, so the question arose on our drive there, "What do prisoners talk about?" He found out.

As we were getting started, an inmate from Cleveland let everyone know how well his football team is doing (1 – 1 – 1). During discussion of their journaling assignment—What do I value?—another complained about his new cellie, a younger man whom he said he needed to train on cellmate etiquette. The inmates got into a discussion of what candy and snacks are their favorites when the get their every other week commissary visit and complained about prices.

I would say the most common topic to pop up is families. Via phone, some endeavor to remain the head of their households; they often talk of their family frustrations. Others talk in anticipation of seeing family members again, either at visitation or upon release. A couple of inmates in particular often mention needing to talk to their mothers to keep them calm and to stay on the straight and narrow.

## Reading Aloud in Prison
### (POSTED 23 AUGUST 2018)

In my project, there are two new items in each weekly workbook section that get read aloud that night. One item each week is from songs with prison-of-my-own-making lyrics. The other is one or two pages on topics such as anger, shame, forgiveness, etc.

For my first few sessions in 2016, I did the reading, thinking the inmates may not like being singled out to recite. Quickly, some inmates volunteered to read. Worried about them struggling, I relaxed after hearing them skate over words such as physiological, frenetically, gravitational and the like.

Inmates' reading levels vary—some have master's degrees, some are having difficulty obtaining GEDs. One named Charles in particular told me a number of times that he had not done the assigned weekly reading because of his lack of reading proficiency.

In about the sixth of the eight sessions, Charles volunteered to read aloud. I was surprised not only because of his acknowledged difficulty reading, but also because his worrying temperament left me thinking he would not want to be in the spotlight anyway.

The other inmates started giving him grief. He bore up under the increased pressure and weighed in. Charles now owes an apology to the English language, but he was tenacious. We applauded when he finished.

## "I Never Thought I'd be Happy to See these Prison Walls."
### (POSTED 28 JUNE 2018)

One of the inmates, Howard, had his birthday while I was out for surgery. So, seeing him this week, I asked, "Howard, How was your birthday?"

He said he spent it at OSU hospital where he was taken to treat a life-threatening condition, retroperistalsis. Having worried that he might not have survived, he then said while throwing his arms up in a hallelujah gesture, "I never thought I'd be so happy to see these prison walls."

## Black and White Thinking in Prison
### (POSTED 11 JUNE 2018)

We got on the topic of white lies or other-centered, prosocial lying which typically occurs as a way of avoiding unpleasant situations or to spare the feelings of whoever is hearing the lie. There is research establishing this behavior can be driven by compassion for the one lied to. (See, Psychology Today, Romeo Vitelli Ph.D., Telling "Little White Lies.")

Elaborating on our theme of the wisdom of "Love thy neighbor as thyself," we focused on the notion of loving, or more simply, accepting, "thyself," despite our flaws and actions such as white lies. I took the position that compassion can drive us to lie to spare the feelings of others, especially, someone not yet strong enough to hear the raw truth. I said confidently, "We all tell whites lies, right?"

I did not expect the pushback that white lies are not only immoral but absent from the behavioral repertoire of most of my inmates. No one openly agreed with me, and most openly and strongly disagreed with me.

My seemingly arguing for lying and my inmates arguing against even the most innocent lie was sharply ironic. Black and white, or dichotomous, thinking causes cognitive distortion forcing viewpoints into either/ or when life just isn't that simple.

## Sleepless in Prison
### (POSTED 29 MARCH 2018)

This week's session included a discussion of forgiveness. Before we even weighed into the topic, one of the inmates talked about how at night, when unable to sleep, all the bad things he did come back to mind for him. That turned out to be a good lead-in to our discussion of forgiveness.

I explained why those sleepless moments of cringe-worthy-ness (See, *Cringeworthy: A Theory of Awkwardness*, M. Dahl.) were good opportunities to practice forgiveness. I paraphrased the following words of Fr. Richard Rohr,

"If you have forgiven yourself for being imperfect, you can now do it for everybody else, too. If you have *not* forgiven yourself, I am afraid you will likely pass on your sadness, absurdity, judgment, and futility to others. 'What goes around comes around.'"

They looked at me as if I were a UFO. Forgiving others, they understood—even though they struggle in practice. Forgiveness of themselves was not something they ever even considered.

So, I challenged them to experiment by using those sleepless, cringe-worthy moments as opportunities to forgive themselves and, eventually, others. And, to report back next week. We will see.

### The Best Drug I Never Used Landed Me in Prison
#### (POSTED 18 MARCH 2018)

I was working with just three of my Level 1 inmates this week. (Things rarely go as planned in Prison work.) They all had earlier held positions of significance in their work. All three were first time drug trafficking felons. None were users of the drugs they sold!

In response to my surprised look, one said, "Are you kidding me? That shit will kill you." For them, the feeling of significance their "drug lord" status gave them in their neighborhoods was their high, their drug, their addiction.

### Any Prisoner's Fear: the Job Interview
#### (POSTED 26 FEBRUARY 2018)

My inmates often express their fears in handling job interviews once they are released. Understandably, their records are going to come up, but how to be truthful and minimize interviewers' concerns is daunting. (Ironically, many of these inmates were entrepreneurs: managing manufacturing, distribution, cash, etc., albeit in illegal enterprises.)

Prison is always full of surprises; I had a new twist on this theme recently. An inmate named Marcos expressed concern about handling job interviews, but as the interviewer! He was going back to a substantial, family manufacturing business with capabilities in laser cutting, stamping, welding and powder coating.

Credibly interviewing job candidates was his top concern. He expressed a "Who-am-I-to-be-asking-you-to-prove-yourself?" angst.

## Drug Logic in Prison
(POSTED 28 MARCH 2019)

Eddie, one of my current inmates was earlier in our program, left prison having completed his sentence, and was reincarcerated in just 16 months. Same offense, drug trafficking.

When I showed my surprise, Eddie explained. Here's his logic.

When he got out, he first landed a low-wage job and, later, a decent paying job. But he could not get landlords to rent to him because of his record. So, he lived in his van saving money to buy a house. He worked as many hours as he could and needed to buy and use drugs to sustain his sleep-deprived work ethic. He hated paying so much for the drugs, so he started trafficking again. He got pulled over with 38 grams of drugs, eleven guns, and a lot of cash. Back to prison for Eddie.

# CHAPTER 13

# Stubborn Facts:
# Prison, It's Not Just for Them

*Mercy without justice is the mother of dissolution;*
*justice without mercy is cruelty.*

THOMAS AQUINAS.

Before my work on the Prison Response-Ability Project, prison and prisoners were out-of-sight out-of-mind for me. What did incarceration have to do with me?

Once I started looking at the numbers in and about prison, I began to think more about what OUR policy is. OUR, as in we are fellow citizens whose country and state enact policies and behave in certain ways that should reflect our values and beliefs.

## Prison, it's Not Just for Them
### (POSTED 23 JUNE 2017)

Before I started working at Lebanon Correctional, prison and prisoners were completely other to me. Out there in the desert of my awareness. In just the last year though, four friends—who are in the same demographic as I—have discussed what it's like to have a relative in prison.

One has a brother who served a year in the 80's for $35 of marijuana. Employability remains a problem to this day.

Another's looked-up-to older brother is in long-term incarceration, setting aside the time he escaped.

A third has a nephew who the last time he was released had so much difficulty adjusting that he robbed a bank, walked out with the money, dropped it in a garbage receptacle, knelt down and waited for the police.

Finally, a friend's father, a building materials salesman, was caught on tape incidental to a RICO investigation. He was incarcerated at age 72.

## Parents in Prison
### (POSTED 20 DECEMBER 2016)

We had an outsider speaking to our Catholic Studies group recently and he asked our inmates who were parents to raise their hands.

I just can't describe my feelings when I saw the vast majority of the inmates raise their hands. After not much research I found a statistic in a September 2016 Cincinnati Enquirer article, "Today, 1 in 14 children have a parent behind bars." Over 7% of our children have an incarcerated parent.

The Enquirer article went on, "And children with incarcerated parents are more likely to have problems in school and to suffer from poor mental and physical health."

## How Did You Get Put in Prison?
### (POSTED 23 MARCH 2017)

I often find myself talking with colleagues about one or the other of the inmates in the project. The colleagues' natural curiosity raises the question, "What crime did he commit?" Surprisingly, I have always had to say, "I don't know."

Early on, I got the sense that being direct and asking, "What did you do to get put in this place?" was out of bounds. Going in, I figured such a question to be trying to get to know someone better. You know, like asking, "Tell me about yourself?" Luckily, since my focus is on their futures and not their pasts, I did not blunder in with the wrong question.

Eventually I understood the rule. "How did you get put in this place?" is the equivalent of asking, "Tell me the worst and most embarrassing thing you ever did?"

I imagined what life would be like if I were continually asked, "Tell me something terrible about yourself?" Then, I remembered that 95% of the 2.3 million people in US prisons will get out and presumably need to get jobs. So, I tried to imagine how a released felon would prepare to discuss in a job interview the worst things he had ever done.

## Let's Spend More Money on Policing and Less on Prison
### (POSTED 18 OCTOBER 2018)

Voting *Yes* on Ballot Issue #1 this November 6th would, among other things, permit inmates to reduce their sentences by up to 25% for participation in rehabilitative, work, or educational programming (except for murder, rape, or child molestation). The measure would also reduce certain drug possession offenses to misdemeanors.

Based on the U.S. Department of Justice's research and my own years of experience volunteering in educational programming at Lebanon Correctional, I will vote to pass the amendment.

Type these words in your internet browser…US DEPARTMENT OF JUSTICE FIVE THINGS ABOUT DETERRENCE. You will learn the following and I think you too will vote to pass the amendment:

1. The *certainty* of being caught is a vastly more powerful deterrent than the punishment.
2. Sending an individual convicted of a crime to prison isn't a very effective way to deter crime.
3. Police deter crime by increasing the perception that criminals will be caught and punished.
4. Increasing the severity of punishment does little to deter crime.
5. There is no proof that the death penalty deters criminals.

Prisons and the death penalty are expensive penalties. Policing reduces the need for penalties.

## Just Showing Up In Prison
### (POSTED 18 APRIL 2018)

Studies show that prison inmates who receive more visits have a greater chance of never returning to prison. Thus, studies suggest that mere contact with the outside community while incarcerated may be rehabilitative. No surprise, merely showing up is good for inmates' socialization.

I started a new group of 14 inmates. This week was our second session. I observed an interesting difference in the prisoners between these two sessions.

Picture three 3ft. × 8ft. cafeteria folding tables lined up to make one big 9ft. × 8ft. surface. In session 1, where most of the inmates had never seen me before, the first to come into the room sat as far away from me as they could. So, the first 12 arrivals left me isolated on one side of the tables. The last 2 of the 14 had to sit on my side of the tables, flanking me.

In session 2, the whole situation was more relaxed and socially appropriate. As they filed in, a couple of them sat next to me and most of them sat nearer than last time. The last man in had to sit the farthest away from me.

## Prison Serial Numbers
### (POSTED 31 JANUARY 2017)

Yes, prisoners in my Prison Response-Ability Project do have serial numbers. Here is a series of other prison numbers of interest:

6 foot × 8 foot…the size of a cell

2…the number of inmates per cell, except for cell block G

2.3 million…the number of prisoners in the US currently

200,000…the number of prisoners in the US in 1972

5×…the current incarceration rate in the US compared to 1970

The same…the US crime rate currently and in 1970

5%…the percent of the world's total population that the US represents

25%…the percent of the world's prison population that the US prison population represents

800%…how much higher the US incarceration rate is compared to, e.g., Germany

16%…the percent of Ohioans who have a criminal record

## What Our Government Knows About Long Prison Sentences
### (POSTED 11 SEPTEMBER 2017)

A Department of Justice agency, the National Institute of Justice, www. nij.gov, has summarized a large body of research on how best to deter crime, as follows:

1. The CERTAINTY of being caught is a vastly more powerful deterrent than the punishment.

2. Sending an individual convicted of a crime to prison isn't a very effective way to deter crime.

3. Police deter crime by increasing the perception that criminals will be caught and punished.

4. Increasing the SEVERITY of punishment does little to deter crime.

5. There is no proof that the death penalty deters criminals.

In short, the research shows that more prison time does not "chasten" individuals convicted of crimes and that prisons may exacerbate recidivism. Moreover, shifting resources from long and costly incarcerations and from the expensive prosecutions of death penalty cases could free up funds for police to increase the certainty of being caught in the minds of criminals and in reality. (Search, "National Institute of Justice Five Things About Deterrence")

## What is the Purpose of Prison?
### (POSTED 7 SEPTEMBER 2017)

Working at Lebanon Correctional presenting my Prison Response-Ability Project, I've begun to wonder if we've actually thought about what we are trying to accomplish with our approach to incarcerating offenders. Some basic concepts come to mind.

**Parole**: a temporary release of a prisoner before the completion of the maximum sentence period requiring agreement to certain conditions.

**Justice**: the rendering to someone what is due.

**Revenge**: to inflict harm in return for a wrongdoing.

**Retributive Justice**: a theory of justice concerned with punishment for wrongdoing. Implicitly, deterrence of crimes or rehabilitation of the offender are not the intent.

**Restorative Justice**: an approach to justice focusing on restoring what is good and, necessarily, meeting the needs of victims, offenders and the community. Victims take an active role in mediating solutions;

offenders take meaningful responsibility for their actions, having the opportunity to right their wrongs and redeem themselves.

Having nearly 1% of our fellow adult US citizens incarcerated or, in total, having nearly 3% of our adult fellow US citizens incarcerated or on probation suggests we should think about what we are trying to accomplish and whether we are succeeding.

## And You Can Be That Servant

If you are thinking about what you can do to give more than you get, I offer the following quote from one of Martin Luther King's last sermons.

"You don't have to have a college degree to serve. You don't have to make your verb and subject agree to serve. You don't have to know about Plato and Aristotle to serve. You don't have to know Einstein's theory of relativity to serve. You need only a heart full of grace. A soul generated by love. And you can be that servant."

# Banned by the Bishop

After three years of weekly visits to Lebanon Correctional Institute presenting The Prison Response-Ability Project and over 130 Facebook/ Linkedin posts, this is my last post.

## Rolling Out In Prison
### (POSTED ON 17 JUNE 2019)

Prison inmates in Ohio are subject to an annual security review which, best case, results in "rolling out" to a lower level of security prison. I understand that Lebanon Correctional is planning construction work on cell blocks and, as a result, is rolling out more inmates than usual. I assume the idea is to roll out a number of inmates equal to one cell block, freeing up a block at a time to work on.

This has clearly left the inmates in the Catholic Studies unsettled. The remaining inmates know they are losing some of the best of them. An inmate gets rolled out based on good behavior.

With this backdrop, I was greatly pained to let the inmates know that this week is my last week at Lebanon Correctional. I, too, have been rolled out. But, in my case, it's for bad behavior.

The Catholic Archdiocese has concluded teaching self-responsibility through the Enneagram is not dogmatically correct. I've read different explanations and best I can tell is that self-awareness of one's Enneagram type may weaken one's conscience. In simpler words, Enneagram knowl-edge would in effect permit a sinner to say, "The devil (my personality) made me do it."

# About the Author

Tom is a partner in a business consultancy in Cincinnati, Ohio. He earned a BS from Denison University and a JD from Salmon P. Chase College of Law, NKU. Tom is a Senior Member of the The Enneagram In Business Network and a Certified Teacher in The Narrative Enneagram.

This, his first book, grew out of years of volunteer work in Lebanon Correctional Institute in Ohio. An executive coach, Tom uses the Enneagram personality model both in and out of prison. The word response-ability simply describes his objective, to enable inmates to respond thoughtfully rather than react impulsively to life's challenges.

Tom entered prison under the auspices of the Catholic Archdiocese of Cincinnati beginning in June 2016. He volunteered weekly in Catholic Programming at Lebanon Correctional. As this book was in its final edit, Tom was informed that the Bishop was banning Tom's work from the program declaring his Enneagram use as inconsistent with Catholic dogma.

CPSIA information can be obtained
at www.ICGtesting.com
Printed in the USA
BVHW051114160523
664253BV00017B/1181